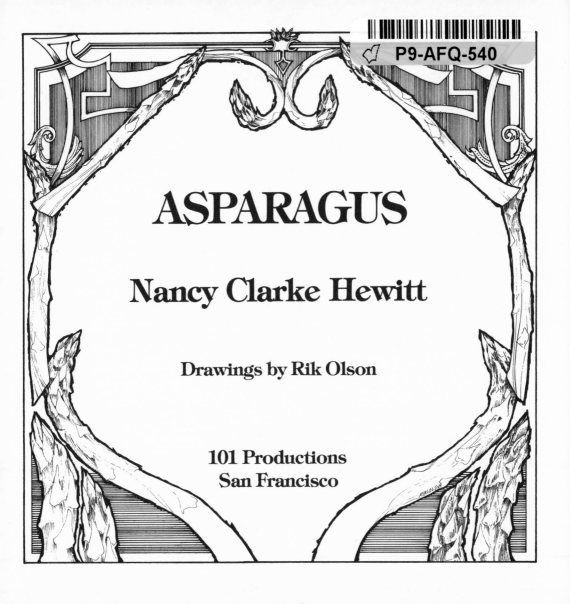

ASPARAGUS

Nancy Clarke Hewitt

Drawings by Rik Olson

101 Productions
San Francisco

To David, Marcella, Ted, Dorothy,
Maggie, Bill D. and Mr. "A"
for their encouragement and shared knowledge

Distributed to the book trade in the United States
by Charles Scribner's Sons, New York, and in Canada
by Van Nostrand Reinhold Ltd., Toronto

Published by 101 Productions
834 Mission Street
San Francisco, California 94103

Library of Congress Cataloging in Publication Data

Hewitt, Nancy Clarke, 1939-
   Asparagus.

   (Edible garden series)
   Includes index.
   1. Cookery (Asparagus)   2. Asparagus.   I. Title.
II. Series.
TX803.A8H48   641.6'5'31   77-3483
ISBN 0-89286-114-2 pbk.

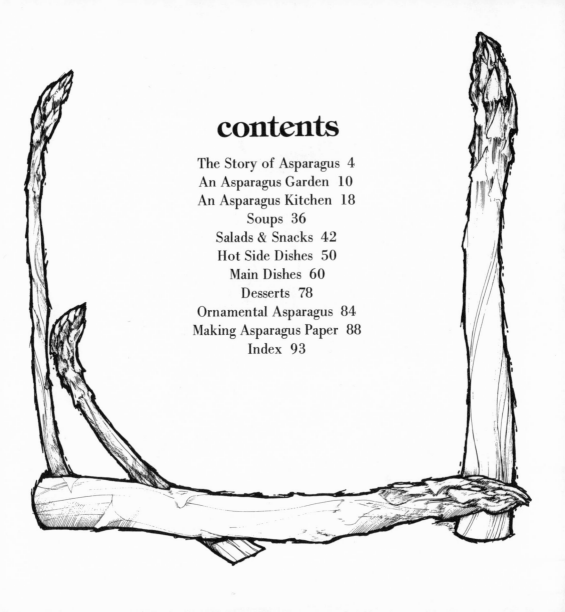

contents

the story of asparagus

The cultivation of *Asparagus officinalis* has a recorded history of more than 2,000 years, but the plant was known for centuries before that. Then, as now, it grew wild in many seacoast areas of Europe. The early gardens of Rome were utilitarian ones with only a few plants added for their particular color or fragrance. The wild asparagus plant soon became part of the kitchen gardens of the ancient Romans, who preferred asparagus cooked just as we do now: rapidly, tender, but not overdone. "Do it quicker than you cook asparagus" was a common Latin saying.

In the 1600's, French royalty, desirous of out-of-season asparagus, had their gardeners "force" asparagus for special banquets. Forcing out-of-season growth is done by the application of artificial heat. The early French "hot beds" were kept in "stove houses," the forerunner of today's greenhouse or hothouse culture, our only source of out-of-season produce until recent years.

Early settlers to America brought asparagus not only to grow as a springtime vegetable, but because they thought it had medicinal properties. Old herbals recording remedies for ailments of every description describe asparagus as a diuretic, a property people believed could cure jaundice. At the same time, however, it was this diuretic nature of asparagus that people believed would cause damage to the kidneys.

In the early 18th century, the Germans began cultivating "white" asparagus. This is done by blanching the stalks: The crown of the plant is placed in a trench and covered with soil. As the tips of the stalks emerge from the earth, the farmer continues to mound the soil around them, admitting no light and resulting in the stalks being bleached of color when harvested.

For the last 30 years in the United States, green asparagus has been generally preferred over the blanched. Nutrition and lower labor costs have both played a role in this preference. The work of blanching asparagus is time-consuming and thus costly. Studies in nutrition show that green asparagus is much higher in food value than white: One cup of cooked green asparagus contains 1,940 units of vitamin A, while the same amount of white stalks has only 190 units. In every cup of cooked green asparagus there are 4.6 milligrams of iron, a mineral difficult to amass without dietary supplements, while the same amount of white asparagus has only 2.4 milligrams.

Asparagus is as beautiful as it is nutritious and it has always had great aesthetic appeal for the artist. Edouard Manet, the French impressionist, painted a small canvas with a bunch of asparagus as its subject. It drew the attention of a patron, who paid much more than the asked-for price. Manet, delighted that someone shared his feeling for his first vegetable portrait, sent as thanks a small painting of a single asparagus stalk, claiming it was missing from the earlier painting. This single stalk had completely different coloring, for it was a different variety. The patron, of course, was delighted.

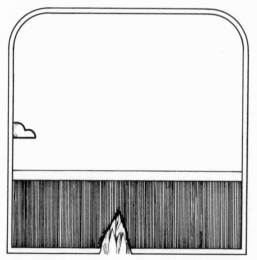 

THE ASPARAGUS INDUSTRY: THE FARM AND THE PACKING HOUSE

Sunnyside, Washington, is one of the small towns of the Yakima Valley in the eastern part of the state. The valley is a large produce growing area, and among the crops grown on the farms here is asparagus. The soil is powder-fine and you have the feeling that a strong wind could blow it all to the next county. On a hot June day a few years ago, I went to Sunnyside, a center of the asparagus industry, to see the farming, harvesting and packing of this crop.

In this valley there is a highly respected farmer, whose innovative ideas have benefited the asparagus industry. He is called "Mr. Asparagus" or "King of Grass" by the community, and he has been farming "grass" since the mid-fifties. (The term "grass" derives from the use of sparrow-grass or its shortened form, "grass," the common appellation for asparagus until the 20th century when the botanical name assumed everyday use. In cookbooks, asparagus is still sometimes referred to as "grass.")

On his farm everything is done to make the harvest time as efficient as possible. The fields are kept weed free; weeding is continued throughout the growing season, and it is performed in the most extraordinary way. On this 55-acre asparagus farm there are 55 geese. It is geese who keep the water and quack grass out of the fields. As long as there are plenty of red berries on the mature asparagus and there is water, the geese will sustain themselves very well.

In recent years Mr. Asparagus has been using an organic fertilizer composed of marine fossil material which is mined in Colorado. He believes this organic material makes for a more tender asparagus stalk. For the consumer, this means more of the stalk can be eaten. There is also an absence of mechanical cutting machines on this farm. The harvest is hand cut because mechanical cutters, by keeping the soil in constant motion as they move down the rows, can damage the as yet unseen stalks below ground level.

When the harvest is over, the area between the rows is cultivated by machine, and the stalks are allowed to grow to maturity. In a few weeks the mature asparagus plumes will cover the fields in a three- to four-foot feathery mass, and then irrigation will begin. With the rows protected from the sun by the plumes, weeds will not grow and evaporation of water will be reduced. In the spring irrigation is used when needed, but most asparagus fields are located in areas where subterranean moisture is sufficient to sustain the fields.

THE PACKING HOUSE

Because asparagus cutting begins just before sunrise and the field work is usually completed by noon, the asparagus arrives at the packing house early in the day. It is first plunged into large vats of ice water, which maintains freshness and cleans the vegetable. Then the company grader evaluates a box of asparagus at random from each farmer's daily harvest. Asparagus is graded according to the amount of green stalk that can be used. Stalks graded "number one" show approximately seven inches of green and two inches of white and receive the best price per pound.

While the grading is underway, the asparagus is lifted from the vats and fed onto conveyor belts. Workers wearing large white cotton gloves keep the asparagus in place before it reaches the trimmer. The trimmer is a circular blade which cuts the butts, or ends, off the asparagus at predetermined lengths. These butts are then given to the farmers for cattle feed.

The asparagus is packed into trapezoidal-shaped shipping crates, the bottom being wider than the top. Each crate holds 30 to 33 pounds of asparagus, and at the wide bottom where the butt end rests there is a thick fiber mat. After the crate is closed it is placed on a conveyor belt that carries it to the shipping dock. This belt travels through a shallow trough of water; the fiber mat absorbs the water and keeps the asparagus fresh and moist for the remainder of the journey.

Asparagus is a member of the lily family, and shares with the tulip, hyacinth and scilla the characteristic of growing after it is cut. With this final spurt of growth, the asparagus will fill the crate before it reaches market, and the consumer.

IN SEARCH OF WILD ASPARAGUS

I can remember the row of asparagus on the west side of my grandparents' garden. The time of the year I enjoyed best was when the lush green plumes of the plants hung heavy with little berries, like a Christmas tree. My grandparents' asparagus plants were refugees from another garden. They had escaped as seed, carried by the wind, or perhaps they came as a piece of root that found its way into the garden soil. You can find your own "escaped" asparagus in the orchards and roadsides near commercial asparagus fields. These are good places to hunt wild asparagus for your table, just as you would hunt wild berries, or mushrooms. They will be hidden in with the tall grasses and other shrubbery. These companion plants form a mulch for the shallow roots of the asparagus plant, keeping the moisture in and the hot sun out, and assuring you of a bountiful harvest.

an asparagus garden

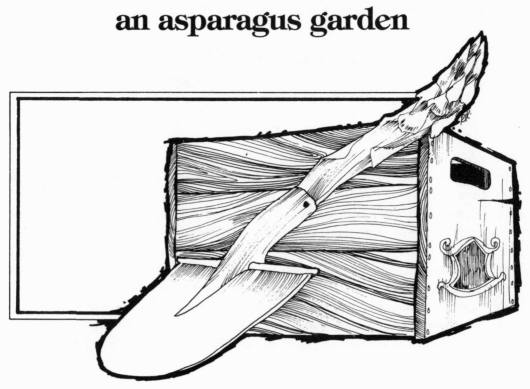

Growing asparagus is a major commitment of both garden space and the gardener's labor and time. You will need many plants to keep even an average-size household contented. Because of the size of the mature individual plants a substantial part of even a large garden will be devoted to this crop. You will also have to wait for 3 to 5 years before you can enjoy a full harvest of your asparagus bed. But there are rewards: The initial labor of preparing the soil and planting will result in a bed that can last anywhere from 10 to 20 years, and after 10 years or so you can start planting new crowns so that the next time the wait will not be noticed. But the greatest reward, of course, is tender young asparagus, just picked from the garden, a freshness that no market-purchased asparagus can match.

There are many asparagus varieties available for the home gardener. Early European varieties boast colorful names indicating size, color, geographical source, such as German Giant, Yellow Burgundy and Argenteuil. In the United States, Mary Washington is an old favorite, and there are other very good varieties available: Waltham Washington, California 500, California 7-11 and Paradise. You can also select from early and late season varieties. All of these varieties are widely available through garden catalogs and garden centers. It is a good idea to seek the advice of your nurseryperson or the local agricultural station on which variety would do best in your particular geographical area.

Though asparagus can be started from seed, the process is slow and tedious and the results are often unsatisfactory. It is best to purchase asparagus crowns, available either 1 or 2 years old. These crowns, which are root clusters, are grown in a "nursery," a small area reserved for starting seeds by commercial growers. As the growth matures, each crown is selected to be transplanted into the asparagus fields or sold to a retail outlet for home gardeners to purchase. Many gardeners prefer the 1-year crowns over the 2-year ones as they are less costly and have lost proportionately less roots when taken from the "nursery" field.

Because an asparagus planting is a permanent addition to the garden, the location must be carefully chosen. The bed should be located at the end of the garden, preferably grouped with other perennials so that cultivation of annuals does not become difficult. Of course, the summer plumage of an asparagus bed makes an excellent complement to a border garden of annual-perennial mix, so you may decide to let beauty override convenience. If the area chosen also has evergreens growing, be sure they do not prevent the new stalks from receiving ample sun during spring growth: An asparagus bed needs full sun for best production.

The soil in the area should be light in texture, a slightly sandy loam that is quick draining. The ground must be well prepared before planting the crowns and it is best to begin working the soil the autumn before you plant if possible, to create an enriched, weed-free growing area. Rid the earth of all stones and twigs, which might cause the development of irregular stalks. Dig the earth well and deeply to aerate the soil and break up any clods. It is at this point that a thorough weeding should be done as weeds are very difficult to control in the young asparagus bed. You should also enrich the soil by digging in some well-rotted manure or compost or any organic matter such as peat moss, bone meal, etc.; this is important because of the long duration of the bed, and because only shallow cultivation will be possible once the bed is established. If your soil tends to be acid, work in some lime to create a correct balance.

Asparagus crowns can be planted in rows about 2 to 3 feet apart or randomly, with anywhere from 6 to 18 inches between the crowns. If you decide to plant the crowns close together, the stalks produced will not be as large, and you will need to compensate for the gain in space by lavish feeding and intense cultivation. The roots of the asparagus plant spread dramatically over the 10- to 20-year life of the bed, and this must be considered. You may decide to plant catch crops between the rows to use the space more economically once the asparagus stalks have been harvested. This will keep down weeds and enrich the soil when the crops are dug under.

Allow about 12 crowns for each individual for 1 or 2 servings of asparagus each week. More crowns should be planted per individual if you are planning to freeze some of the harvest for later use.

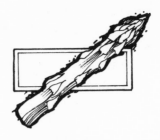

THE FIRST SEASON

In the spring, as soon as the ground can be worked and all danger of frost is past, prepare the soil. Spade to loosen the earth and rake well to eliminate any stray rocks and to break up soil clumps; weed well. Dig deeply into the soil a 5-10-10 fertilizer, mixing in 4 to 5 pounds per 100 square feet. Once the soil is of good consistency, you are ready to plant. Be sure that the soil is prepared as soon as possible in the spring, so that no time is lost once the crowns are purchased.

There are two ways to plant the asparagus crowns: the trench method and the simple shallow planting method. The latter should be attempted only if the soil is very rich and the planting situation near ideal. With this method the crowns are covered with about 3 inches of soil. Dig shallow, wide 3- to 4-inch-deep holes about 6 inches apart and place the crown in the hole, laying the roots flat. Cover with the removed topsoil, mixed with well-rotted compost. Firm the soil well and water deeply. Studies have been done by the University of California in the past few years which have shown this to be a superior planting method for both the home gardener and the commercial asparagus grower, though the latter must allow a greater distance between the plants for mechanical cultivation. I recommend you try this method, especially if your garden space is limited. Remember, though, the plants will need more food and closer attention to cultivation to compensate for the limited volume of the growing medium. Some growers advocate the use of a high-nitrogen fertilizer when using this planting method.

A more common practice is to dig trenches about 10 inches deep and about a foot wide. Put a shallow layer of compost or manure in the bottom of the trenches and cover with an inch of topsoil. Place the crowns in the trenches, spacing them about a foot apart and spreading the roots out evenly. Cover the crowns with about 2 to 3 inches of soil, firming it well, and water deeply. Do not add more soil until shoots appear; then cover the shoots with 2 to 3 more inches of soil. Continue repeating this process until the trenches are filled in completely. Some gardeners prefer to add soil until a slight hill or mound is formed. A mixture of good quality topsoil and humus-rich compost is best for filling in the trenches, and the soil should always be well firmed around the roots with each addition. Always soak the soil deeply when it begins to dry around the root mass.

Continue to water the asparagus plants when you water your vegetables and ornamentals; it is important that the roots never dry out. As the foliage of the asparagus plant matures it blocks the sun from the soil around the base of the plant which helps to keep weeds from sprouting. This same foliage will help keep the moisture in the soil from evaporating. Keep watch, though, and immediately pull any weeds which catch hold.

In this first season, harvest no stalks. Let the stalks go to "fern," and then cut them back in late fall or early winter. Some gardeners leave the stalks as a mulch and also dress the bed with a layer of fresh manure to mulch and enrich the soil. When spring comes you will rake away the straw-like covering and carefully fork the well-decayed manure into the soil, being careful not to damage the roots. Asparagus plants are hearty eaters and will appreciate this nutrient boost. The red berries that form on the foliage should be picked off and discarded as they will produce plants of inferior quality. (While most plants have male and female *parts,* asparagus *plants* are either male or female. The male is the more productive while the female bears the red berries.)

THE SECOND SEASON

Asparagus bed care for the second season starts with top dressing the soil with a 5-10-10 fertilizer. You will be able to harvest some of the stalks produced in this season, but you must exercise restraint. Cut only half or less of the edible stalks produced and cut for only 4 weeks of the season if you want to ensure a well-established bed in the future. Cutting half means that every time you go out to harvest you must take only half of the newly sprouted stalks. The stalks that you did not cut earlier will be too mature to consider for the table. Select stalks that are about 8 inches long. Take the stalk between your thumb and forefinger, a couple of inches above the soil line, press on the spear and it will snap where it is tender. If taken directly to the kitchen for a meal, further trimming of the end is unnecessary. Some gardeners prefer to cut the stalk just below the soil line with an ordinary knife or a specialized asparagus knife. Place the knife next to the spear and run it down in the soil to the desired depth; turn the knife slightly and cut the stalk cleanly. Be careful not to injure any shoots that may be forming beneath the soil.

By this time you will be enthusiastic about asparagus gardening and cooking, and it will be hard to limit yourself to half the harvest. But remember, there is always next year, and if your craving for this vegetable overrules your food budget, mid-October brings asparagus from Mexico and California-grown stalks begin appearing on the produce stands in February. Buying them will be a luxury, but it may be one in which you feel you can indulge.

By the end of the season much of the asparagus patch will be in fern. The asparagus fern must be tended as a foliage plant after the harvest season. This means that one should keep the area well watered during the summer growing season as the asparagus matures and an application of fertilizer should be made. A good summer's growth increases the capacity of the crown and develops root growth, ensuring a healthy cutting season the following year. Within several years, the crown will have grown to 2 feet in diameter and an extensive root system will have developed. Treat the asparagus bed as you did at the end of the first season.

THE THIRD SEASON

This season will be the first one in which a complete cycle of asparagus care and growth has previously occurred. Begin the season with a top dressing of a 5-10-10 fertilizer as soon as your area is frost-free. This third year crop can be harvested until temperatures rise to levels of 70° to 75°, which causes new growth to be tough and fibrous. The traditional date for ending the annual asparagus harvest is June 20, and studies have been done by the University of California which show this date to be applicable for all areas.

Some gardeners feel that even the third season should not be a full harvest one, that again only half of the harvest should be taken or that stalks should be harvested fully for only 4 weeks, or until only smallish stalks are being produced. The way you harvest will depend on the general health and vigor of your bed. You must be careful not to over-harvest your asparagus bed to its future detriment.

FORCING ASPARAGUS

Once you have a mature asparagus bed, at least 5 years old, it is possible to force part of that bed to produce early stalks with the same technique that is used to prompt rhubarb into early growth. In the spring place a wide barrel or wooden box that is open ended over the plants you wish to force. Pile manure or compost around the container, sealing the area where container and soil meet. Then attach a clear plastic tarp or sheet of plastic film that has been perforated for ventilation securely to the top of the barrel or box. Windows salvaged from other structures will also work for this purpose; prop the window open occasionally during the day for air circulation. Depending on the temperature, asparagus can appear in 7 days. Then in about 1 week to 10 days they can be harvested for the table. Rotate the forcing areas of your asparagus bed from year to year, so that the forced plants have a chance to rejuvenate themselves. It is possible to start asparagus in this way 4 to 6 weeks before the asparagus season begins in your area.

BLANCHING ASPARAGUS

If you wish to raise white asparagus, this can be done by heaping soil around the stalks as they emerge from the earth. This will cut off the light from the shoots and the normally green stalk will be white except at the very tip. The soil should be a good, rich mixture of topsoil and well-rotted compost. White asparagus is considered a delicacy by some, and if you intend to grow them, I suggest you select varieties best suited to blanching.

PESTS AND DISEASES

Though asparagus plants do not generally suffer from pest invasions and diseases, the long life of the bed requires the gardener to be on the watch for possible problems. Slugs and snails may decide to invade, in which case pick them off and destroy. Asparagus beetles may feed on the young stalks or the larvae may munch on the berries of the fruiting plants. There are two basic kinds of asparagus beetles: The common variety has a blue-black body with 3 white spots and orange markings on the wings; the larger ones have reddish-brown bodies with 12 white spots and 6 black spots on each wing. The best prevention is a well-tended garden, without any sticks, trash or leaves for the beetles to nest in. The adult beetles can be picked off the plants and destroyed.

Asparagus rust, a disease which forms on the foliage of the asparagus plant, is not the problem it has been in the past. Varieties have been developed which are resistant to this formerly prevalent disease. Among these are the 'Washington' varieties. I would advise growing one of these disease-resistant strains.

an asparagus kitchen

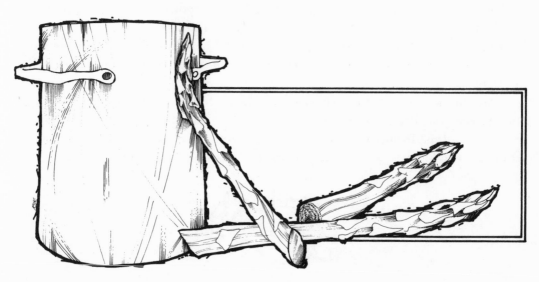

Asparagus is at its sweetest when freshly cut from the plant. Within hours of harvest, the sugars will turn to starches and the asparagus will begin to lose its flavor. Commercial asparagus reaches the market about 5 days after harvest, and if stored for 2 weeks will develop a bitter flavor. Because of this, you should eat commercial asparagus as soon as possible after purchase. If your household has a particularly healthy asparagus appetite, consider buying a 30-pound crate; or share the surplus with friends.

If you have an asparagus patch, cut the stalks when they are about 8 inches in height. If you are purchasing the asparagus, select good-sized stalks with tightly formed tips; these are considered the tenderest. The tips are composed of tiny overlapping scales. On very mature stalks these scales are expanded to reveal a small floret, indicating the spear was too mature when cut. Always check the tip ends to avoid purchasing tough old stalks. The stalk should be moist looking overall and there should be no sign of withering at the butt end.

Asparagus that is to be cooked or frozen some time after harvest should be refrigerated. It should never be snapped, cut or cleaned until it is time to prepare it for the table or the freezer. Asparagus wrapped in plastic bags or in slightly moist towels and placed in the crisper of a refrigerator will keep its texture adequately for several days. You can also store it upright: Place the butt ends in 1-inch-deep water and cover the stalks with a plastic bag.

White asparagus must always be peeled before cooking. In general I feel the peeling of any green asparagus is unnecessary, though many cooks feel peeling the stalks is worth the extra effort. Young tender green asparagus is generally not peeled if it is cooked by steaming in an upright position, as the tips will cook more slowly than the butt ends. If however, the asparagus is being steamed in a horizontal position, or if it is being cooked by the French-style boiling water method it is recommended by many that it be peeled. This is because the whole stalk will be cooking in the same amount of time, and peeling will prevent overcooking of the tips. Peeled asparagus also cooks more quickly than unpeeled, and peeling allows one to eat the entire stalk, rather than losing 1 or 2 inches at the butt end because the outer flesh is too fibrous.

If you are not peeling the stalks, begin by snapping off the butt ends: The tender portion of the stalk will bend easily and break from the fibrous end. If you are peeling the stalks, cut only about 1/2 inch off the butt end. Place the asparagus in a sink or a container filled with cool water and move the stalks through the water to loosen any sand or soil. Rinse the stalks, checking the tip ends carefully to be sure no grit or soil has clung to the scales. Using a vegetable peeler, sharp knife or asparagus scaler, begin at the butt end of the stalk and shave each stalk to within about 2 inches of the tip end. You should remove more of the fibrous flesh at the butt end and only lightly shave the more tender tip end. Place the stalks in a bowl of cold water as you finish peeling them.

Do not discard the fibrous ends you have snapped off. They can be used either for making stocks or soups or for papermaking (see Making Asparagus Paper). Keep the ends well wrapped in the refrigerator or freezer until ready to use.

COOKING ASPARAGUS

Various vessels can be used for cooking asparagus. Specially designed asparagus steamers are available in two basic shapes: One holds the asparagus upright, while the other holds them horizontally. These cookers have baskets or liners which hold the asparagus above the steaming water. You can, however, fabricate an asparagus steamer from a double boiler by placing the asparagus in the bottom pan, with tips facing up, and inverting the top pan over them. A drip coffee pot with the insides removed may also be used. With either of these, though, the butt ends of the stalks will be *resting in* 1 to 2 inches of water. A collapsible steaming basket that can be placed in pans of different sizes is good for steaming small amounts of asparagus.

If you are cooking a large amount of stalks, group them according to thickness and form them into bundles of about 10 to 12 stalks; secure the bundles with soft string just below the tips and at the butt ends. All of the ends should be trimmed to the same length. Place the bundles in the basket or liner of an asparagus steamer (or in a fabricated one as described above), and pour water to 1-inch depth in the bottom of the steamer. Cover and bring to a boil and cook for about 10 to 15 minutes, depending upon the thickness of the stalks. Some cooks prefer putting in a single loose stalk, so that it can be tested for doneness without having to disturb the bundles. The asparagus is done when you can pierce the largest part of the stalk with a knife tip.

An alternative French-style method for cooking asparagus uses a pan large enough to hold a substantial amount of water. Fill the container two-thirds full with salted water (1-1/2 teaspoons salt per quart of water) and bring to a rolling boil. Drop in the asparagus bundles, and timing from when the water returns to a boil, cook uncovered for 6 to 8 minutes, depending on the thickness of the stalks. Test for doneness with a knife tip, and again a single loose stalk can be placed in the pot to facilitate testing. Though with this boiling method there is a greater loss of nutrients, the asparagus retains a vibrant green color and good texture.

If you are cooking only a small amount of asparagus, the bundling will become unnecessary, and you may choose to cook it loose in a skillet with a very small amount of water. It is best to keep the water simmering and to cook the asparagus uncovered to maintain its fresh color.

My favorite vessel for cooking asparagus is a spaghetti cooker. I simply place the stalks, unbundled, vertically in the basket, put about 1 inch of water in the bottom of the pot, lower the basket into it and steam the stalks until they are cooked al dente, about 10 minutes. This method works well if you are cooking a large amount of asparagus that will snugly fill the basket.

When the asparagus has finished cooking (cut the strings from the bundles if they are bundled), drain the stalks by placing them on a cloth napkin to absorb excess moisture or on an asparagus serving platter with a perforated liner. If you are serving the asparagus cold, place it under cold running water for 1 to 2 minutes or put it in a bowl of ice water, as this will stop the cooking immediately. Then drain it well. Properly cooked asparagus will be firm but tender, and never limp; it will be *al dente*—resistant to the bite. Save any cooking water for use in soups and stocks. An additional hint: When cooking asparagus for the evening meal, cook more than is needed, for use in other recipes.

SERVING PORTIONS
Allow 1/3 to 1/2 pound of asparagus stalks for each serving. There are generally 14 to 18 medium-size asparagus stalks per pound, about 24 of the thinner stalks.

PRESERVING ASPARAGUS
Freezing is the most desirable way to preserve asparagus at home. Canning asparagus is expensive and time consuming, and both texture and taste are very different from fresh or frozen asparagus. If you have your own asparagus bed, you can simplify the freezing process by freezing part of your crop each day you harvest. Harvest all of the asparagus that is ready, use what you need for your meal that day, and then freeze the surplus in serving-size portions.

Select young tender asparagus of good color with compact tips. Clean and peel asparagus and prepare bundles as described in Cooking Asparagus. Bring a large pot of water to a rolling boil (1 gallon of water for each pound of asparagus) and lower the bundles into the water. Timing from the moment the water returns to the boil, blanch the asparagus 3 minutes. Lift the bundles from the pot and plunge them into ice water to stop the cooking; drain well and let cool until they can be easily handled. Then chill the asparagus stalks until they have cooled completely and pack in airtight containers: plastic bags, foil or plastic freezer containers. Label and date the containers, specifying the amount in each package, and freeze until ready to use.

A spaghetti cooker works well for the blanching step, as the asparagus can be placed in the basket of the cooker and easily lowered into and removed from the water.

An alternative method is to steam-blanch the asparagus, not more than a pound at a time, by placing stalks above boiling water and steaming them for 4 minutes. Then plunge them into ice water and proceed as directed for the blanching method described above.

Asparagus can also be packed for freezing by the loose-pack method. When the blanched asparagus has cooled completely, place the stalks on cookie sheets, making sure they are not touching. Place the cookie sheets in the freezer for a few hours until the stalks are frozen. Bundle the stalks in the desired-size portions and place in containers or wrapping for freezing. Label and freeze as described above.

Sun-drying is the oldest method of preserving asparagus. Now, however, there are machines available which can be used in the home for drying all types of fruit and vegetables. If you have one of these machines, consider drying some of your asparagus harvest. Sun-drying is dependent on ideal conditions: full, steady sunlight, very low humidity, good air circulation, pollutant-free air. Oven-drying is also possible, or a combination of sun- and oven-drying can be done: moving the drying trays to the oven when the sun has lost its intensity. The greatest danger with sun-drying asparagus is not being able to dehydrate the vegetable sufficiently before the onset of decomposition. Because of their low-acid content, it is also necessary to steam-blanch asparagus to stop enzymatic action before you begin to dry it; and, too, you will need to construct proper drying trays or even a cold frame-type structure for capturing sufficient heat. In the end, the product you have will not be to the standards of commercially dried asparagus and I would not recommend this method of preserving unless one is completely knowledgeable of the procedure.

If you do decide to dry your asparagus, you will find that when reconstituted it has a texture much like canned asparagus and is brownish in color. Dried asparagus is best used finely ground and added to broths or sauces for flavoring. A tea made from ground dried asparagus is believed to have medicinal value.

STAPLES FOR AN ASPARAGUS KITCHEN

The following are recipes for sauces and condiments to accompany or season asparagus, and techniques for various asparagus preparations.

COARSELY CHOPPED ASPARAGUS AND ASPARAGUS PURÉE

To make coarsely chopped asparagus place 1/2-inch pieces of the stalks in a blender or food processor and chop just until they are finely cut and of dry consistency; do not let them become a paste. This consistency can also be attained by using a good sharp straight-bladed knife and a wooden chopping block or a mincing knife in a wooden bowl.

To make asparagus purée continue to blend the pieces of stalk to the paste stage. Chicken stock, water or any liquid that complements the recipe you are preparing may be added for a smoother-textured purée. An alternate way to prepare asparagus purée, especially if you have neither a blender nor a food processor, is to blanch the stalks for 3 to 4 minutes and then press them through a sieve, ricer or food mill. Approximately 2 cups of chopped asparagus (1/2-inch lengths) will make 1 cup asparagus purée.

ASPARAGUS JUICE

To make asparagus juice put the stalks through a juice extractor. The juice smells and tastes much like fresh green peas. The pulp that is leftover can be saved and used for making paper (see Making Asparagus Paper). One pound of asparagus will yield approximately 1 cup of asparagus juice.

For an unusual seasoning you can always have on hand, mix 1 cup of asparagus juice with 1/2 cup grated cucumber. Freeze in an ice cube tray and use to flavor soups and tomato drinks.

ASPARAGUS STOCK

The liquid that remains from cooking asparagus can be saved, and frozen if desired, to be used for soups, stocks and sauces.

DILL

This herb is used frequently in the recipes in this book. It is usually found fresh at the market in the early fall, but it can also be easily grown in your garden. Mince or snip the dill feathers and divide them into small packets of plastic or foil; a packet should contain an amount suitable for a recipe. Keep several packets in a large container in the freezer for use during the year, when dill is not in season. The flavor of frozen dill is far superior to that of dried.

TAMARI SOY SAUCE

This soy sauce is a naturally fermented flavoring of soybeans , wheat, water and salt. It contains no preservatives, sugar or artificial coloring, which are commonly found in most commercial soy sauce. Tamari soy can be found in health food stores and some supermarkets.

BLENDER HOLLANDAISE SAUCE

4 egg yolks
6 tablespoons sweet butter, melted
   and cooled

2 tablespoons fresh lemon juice
   or to taste
1/8 teaspoon salt

Put the egg yolks in a blender or food processor and blend until smooth. With the motor running, add the butter and lemon juice in a slow steady stream; add salt. Serve immediately or refrigerate for up to 3 or 4 days; bring to room temperature before serving.
Makes about 1 cup

HOLLANDAISE SAUCE

This is a very thick sauce. If you prefer a thinner sauce, more like the classic hollandaise, use only 3 egg yolks.

6 egg yolks
2 tablespoons water
1/4 pound sweet butter, cut into
   small pieces

2 to 3 tablespoons fresh lemon juice
1/4 teaspoon salt
1/8 teaspoon white pepper

Combine the egg yolks and water in a small saucepan and beat well. Place over low heat and, stirring, cook yolks until slightly thickened and creamy. Add butter gradually, beating continuously. Let each piece of butter melt into the yolks as you continue to beat. After sauce thickens add the lemon juice and salt and pepper. This sauce may be served warm or cold.

Makes about 1-1/4 cups

Variations
• Add 1 teaspoon grated lemon zest for a more pronounced lemon flavor.
• Substitute fresh orange juice for the lemon juice and add 1 teaspoon grated orange zest.

MOUSSELINE SAUCE

Whip 1/3 cup heavy cream until stiff and fold into Hollandaise Sauce, preceding.
Makes about 1-2/3 cups

MORNAY SAUCE

1 shallot, minced or
3 green onions, white part only,
    minced
2 tablespoons butter
2 tablespoons flour
1/2 cup vegetable stock, such as
    asparagus or celery, heated

1/2 cup milk, scalded
1 tablespoon heavy cream
1 egg yolk
1/4 cup grated Parmesan or Gruyère
    cheese

In a saucepan sauté the shallot or green onions in the butter until translucent. Blend the flour into the butter mixture and cook over moderate heat, stirring, for about 2 minutes. Slowly add the vegetable stock and milk, stirring constantly. Cook over medium heat, continuing to stir, until sauce is thickened. Beat together the cream and egg yolk and whisk a little bit of the hot sauce into the egg mixture. Then add to the sauce, stirring constantly until the sauce is heated through. Add the cheese and stir and heat just until cheese is melted.
Makes about 1-1/4 cups

BÉCHAMEL SAUCE

2 tablespoons butter
2 tablespoons flour
1/2 cup half-and-half cream or milk

1/2 cup vegetable stock, such as aspara-
    gus or celery, heated
freshly grated nutmeg to taste
salt and white pepper to taste

Melt the butter in a saucepan and blend in the flour. Cook over moderate heat, stirring, 2 minutes. Slowly add the half-and-half cream and vegetable stock, stirring constantly. Cook over moderate heat, continuing to stir until sauce is thickened. Season with salt and white pepper.

Makes about 1 cup

Variations
- Omit the stock and use 1 cup half-and-half cream or milk.
- After the sauce has thickened, whisk a small amount of the sauce into the beaten yolk of 1 egg, add egg mixture to the saucepan and stir until heated through.
- Omit nutmeg and add 1 to 2 tablespoons fresh lemon juice just before removing from the heat.

RICE SAUCE

1-1/4 cups water
1/2 cup rice
3 whole allspice
1/4 teaspoon ground mace

freshly grated nutmeg to taste
1 cup milk
1/4 cup heavy cream
salt to taste

Bring water to a boil, add rice and spices and reduce to a simmer; cover and cook for 40 minutes, stirring occasionally. A few minutes before rice is done, mix milk and cream and heat to a simmer. Put the rice and the heated milk and cream into a blender and blend until smooth. Season with salt to taste. If the sauce is too thick, more milk may be added.

Makes about 2-1/4 cups

BLENDER MAYONNAISE

3 large eggs
1-1/4 cups olive oil
1-3/4 cups corn oil

2 teaspoons fresh lemon juice
1/2 teaspoon salt

Put the eggs into a blender and blend until smooth. With the motor running, slowly add the olive oil and corn oil in a thin, steady stream. Then add lemon juice and salt and blend for 1 minute.
Makes about 3 cups

Orange Mayonnaise Combine 3 tablespoons fresh orange juice, 1 tablespoon grated orange zest and 1 cup mayonnaise. Blend well in a blender.
Garlic Mayonnaise Add 1 garlic clove, minced, to 1 cup mayonnaise. Blend well in a blender.
Curry Mayonnaise Add 1 teaspoon curry powder to 1 cup mayonnaise. Blend well in a blender and add more curry to taste.

GARLIC CHEESE SAUCE

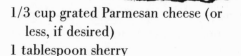

1/2 cup Garlic Mayonnaise, preceding
1/4 cup heavy cream

1/3 cup grated Parmesan cheese (or
   less, if desired)
1 tablespoon sherry

Combine all ingredients in a saucepan and place over low heat until cheese is melted and sauce is heated through. To serve hot, prepare sauce in a chafing dish. May be refrigerated and reheated.
Makes about 1 cup

CELERY SAUCE

1 bunch celery, trimmed and cut in
    1-inch pieces
1 cup water

1 teaspoon fresh lemon juice
salt and freshly ground pepper to taste

Cook celery in water in a saucepan until the celery is very tender but not mushy. Pour celery into a sieve to drain (the liquid may be reserved for use in another recipe). Press the drained celery through the sieve or a food mill and reheat. Add lemon juice and salt and pepper to taste.
Makes about 1 cup

Variation Substitute 1 medium whole celery root, peeled and cut in 1-inch pieces, or 1 pound of Jerusalem artichokes, peeled and cut in 1-inch pieces, for the celery. These vegetables may be puréed in a blender and do not need to be put through a sieve. Add some of the cooking liquid if a thinner sauce is desired. Each of these vegetables will make about 1-1/2 cups of sauce.

NATURAL TOMATO SAUCE

1 onion, chopped
2 tablespoons butter

3 pounds tomatoes, peeled, seeded
    and chopped

In a saucepan sauté the onion in 1 tablespoon of the butter until translucent. Add the tomatoes and simmer uncovered for 30 minutes. Stir in the remaining table-spoon of butter. May be refrigerated or frozen.
Makes about 3 cups

Note A pinch of sugar may be added to the tomato sauce if desired.

FRESH AVOCADO DIP

pulp of 1 large or 3 medium
  avocados

1 tablespoon fresh lemon juice
1/2 teaspoon tamari soy sauce

Combine all ingredients and purée in a blender or food processor. Adjust seasonings.
Makes about 1-1/2 cups

Variations
- Substitute 2 teaspoons or more Hot Stuff, following, for the tamari soy sauce.
- Add peeled, seeded and finely diced tomato.

HOT STUFF

2 green bell peppers, seeded and
  cut up
1 8-ounce can green chili peppers,
  drained
1 cup cider vinegar

1/2 cup fresh lemon juice
4 cups sugar
grated zest of 1 lemon
2 tablespoons minced pimiento
1 6-ounce jar liquid pectin

Put the green peppers and chili peppers in a blender and liquify. Add the vinegar and
lemon juice and blend in well. Put the pepper mixture in a saucepan, add the sugar
and lemon zest and bring to a boil. Continue to boil, stirring constantly, for 4
minutes. Remove from the heat, skim off any foam with a metal spoon and stir in
the pimiento. Mix in the liquid pectin and stir well. Pour into clean glass jars with
tight-fitting lids and refrigerate.
Makes about 7 cups

Note This recipe can also be put into hot, sterilized jelly jars, leaving 1/2-inch headroom, and sealed with a 1/8-inch layer of melted paraffin, in which case refrigeration is not necessary. Mason-type canning jars and lids may also be used. Store in a cool, dark place.

PIE CRUST

1-1/2 cups unbleached flour
1/2 cup whole wheat flour
1 teaspoon sugar
1/2 teaspoon salt

6 tablespoons butter, chilled and cut
  into small pieces
4 tablespoons shortening, chilled and
  cut into small pieces
4 to 6 tablespoons ice water

Combine the flours, sugar and salt in a bowl. With your fingertips, mix the butter and shortening into the flour mixture until a crumbly consistency is formed, much like coarse cornmeal. Sprinkle the mixture with 4 tablespoons of ice water and lightly blend the water into the dough, adding more ice water if necessary to hold the ingredients together. Form dough into a ball, remove to a lightly floured board, knead lightly and flatten slightly into a disc. Cover the dough with plastic wrap and chill it in the refrigerator for at least 30 minutes. On a lightly floured board roll out the dough 1/8 inch thick and fit into a pan as described in recipe.
Makes 1 10- or 12-inch crust

Note For a prebaked crust, fit dough into pan, line with aluminum foil oiled on the bottom side and fill with dried beans or rice. Place in a 400° oven for 8 minutes until crust is set. Remove from the oven and remove foil. Place on a rack to cool.

3 cups unbleached flour
1 teaspoon salt

4 eggs, beaten
1/2 cup asparagus purée

Sift the flour and salt onto a wooden board and make a well in the center. Combine the eggs and asparagus in a blender and blend until smooth (or beat with a whisk until smooth). Put the asparagus mixture into the well formed by the flour and work in the flour with your fingers until a smooth dough is formed. Then knead the dough until very smooth and elastic, about 10 minutes, adding 2 to 4 tablespoons flour as you knead. Cover dough with plastic wrap or a bowl and let rest for at least 10 minutes (20 minutes is better).

To make the noodles by hand, divide the dough into 2 pieces and on a lightly floured board, flatten each of the pieces into an oblong shape with the palm of your hand. Then roll out each piece as thinly as possible by rolling and turning the dough as you work. Sprinkle lightly with flour and let the dough rest for 10 minutes; then roll each portion into a jelly-roll shape and cut the dough into crosswise strips, 1/2-inch wide.

To make the noodles with a pasta machine, divide the dough into 6 pieces. Flatten each piece into an oval and feed through the no. 2 notch on the pasta machine. Then feed each strip through the no. 4 notch, and finally the no. 6 notch. Now run the strips through the wide noodle cutter on the machine.

Once the noodles have been cut, spread them on a clean cloth and let dry for about 1 hour. Then cook them in a large kettle of salted boiling water (1 tablespoon salt per gallon of water) for about 5 to 7 minutes, or until al dente.
Makes about 1 pound fresh noodles

Curry Noodles Substitute 6 eggs and 1/2 cup curry powder for the eggs and asparagus purée. Proceed as directed.

Dill Noodles Substitue 1/2 cup minced dill for the asparagus purée and proceed as directed.

Dried Noodles Lay the noodles on a clean cloth and turn them every few hours until they are completely dry. You may also hang noodles that are over 18 inches in length over the back of a chair or on the handles of wooden spoons that have been secured by closing the bowl of the spoon in a drawer. Do not attempt to dry the noodles in too hot a room or they will crack. Dried noodles will keep for weeks in airtight containers of metal, glass or plastic. This recipe will make about 12 ounces dried noodles.

Note You may decide to cut the noodles in various lengths and/or widths for different uses. These doughs can serve for lasagne noodles (2 inches wide and 6 inches long), tagiatelle noodles (3/4 inch wide), or may be cut in various lengths and widths for use in casseroles and stuffings.

soups

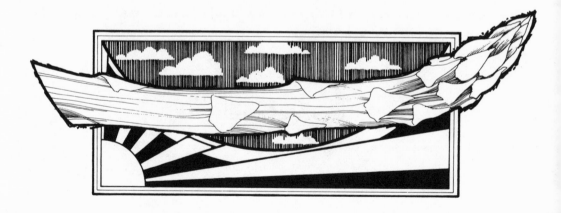

TOMATO-ASPARAGUS SOUP

1 part Natural Tomato Sauce, page 31
1 part rich chicken stock
cooked asparagus, cut into bite-size
    pieces

salt and freshly ground pepper to taste
minced dill or Garlic Mayonnaise,
    page 30, for garnish

Heat together the sauce, stock and asparagus; do not boil. Season with salt and pepper and serve very hot. Garnish each bowl with minced dill or a teaspoon of Garlic Mayonnaise.

Variation Substitute an equal amount of half-and-half cream for half the stock.

CLEAR GREEN SOUP

4 cups rich chicken or turkey stock
1 cup cut-up asparagus (1-inch lengths)
1/2 cup halved snow peas
a few day lily buds, just showing color

2 tablespoons minced green onion
4 tablespoons Fresh Avocado Dip,
    page 32, for garnish

Bring the stock to a simmer, add the asparagus and cook until al dente, about 5 minutes. Add the snow peas, day lily buds and green onion and simmer 2 minutes. Ladle into bowls and garnish each with 1 tablespoon of Fresh Avocado Dip.
Serves 4

ASPARAGUS GAZPACHO

1 pound tomatoes, peeled, seeded and
   coarsely chopped
1/2 cup chopped asparagus
1/2 small green bell pepper (optional)

1 shallot
1/4 teaspoon salt
1/8 teaspoon freshly ground pepper
cucumber sticks and lemon wedges

Combine tomatoes, asparagus, bell pepper, shallot, salt and pepper in a blender and blend until liquified. Chill for several hours. Just before serving, adjust seasonings to taste. Serve with cucumber sticks and lemon wedges.
Serves 3

Variations
- Thin to desired consistency with tomato juice and serve as a beverage.
- Heat and serve as a hot soup.

ASPARAGUS ORANGE SOUP

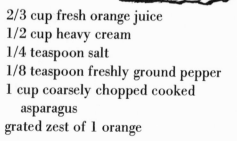

1-1/2 tablespoons butter
1 large shallot, minced
1-1/2 tablespoons unbleached flour
1 cup rich chicken stock, heated
1 cup milk, scalded
2 egg yolks

2/3 cup fresh orange juice
1/2 cup heavy cream
1/4 teaspoon salt
1/8 teaspoon freshly ground pepper
1 cup coarsely chopped cooked
   asparagus
grated zest of 1 orange

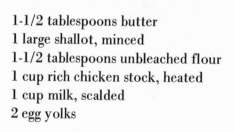

Melt the butter in a saucepan and sauté the shallot until translucent. Sprinkle the flour into the pan and cook and stir for 1 to 2 minutes; do not brown. Gradually stir in the chicken stock and milk and cook on low heat for 10 minutes, stirring occasionally. While milk mixture is cooking, combine the egg yolks, orange juice, cream, salt and pepper in a blender and blend well. Whisk a little of the milk mixture into the egg mixture then slowly add to the milk mixture over low heat, stirring. Add the asparagus and orange zest and heat until very hot, but do not boil. Adjust seasonings. This soup may be served hot or cold.

Serves 4

ASPARAGUS MISO SOUP

6 cups rich turkey or chicken stock
6 tablespoons miso*
1/2 pound asparagus, cut into 1-inch
  pieces

1/2 pound snow peas
alfalfa sprouts for garnish
tamari soy sauce

In a saucepan combine the stock and miso. Bring to a simmer, mixing well. Add the asparagus and continue to simmer until asparagus is al dente, about 5 minutes. Add snow peas and cook 30 seconds, or until just heated through. Serve hot in patterned bowls garnished with alfalfa sprouts. Let each person add tamari soy sauce to taste. Sesame crackers make a nice addition.

Serves 4

*Soybean paste made from fermented soybeans, rice or wheat and salt. The two basic types, red and white, are available packaged in Japanese markets and some supermarkets. Either type may be used for this soup.

ASPARAGUS-WALNUT SOUP

1/2 pound asparagus, cut into
   1/2-inch pieces
3 cups rich chicken stock

1/2 cup walnut halves, finely ground
salt and white pepper to taste

Purée asparagus with 1 cup of the chicken stock in a blender or food processor. Combine in a saucepan with the remaining chicken stock and simmer for 5 minutes. Add the ground nuts and salt and pepper and simmer 2 minutes. Serve hot or chilled.
Serves 3 or 4

ASPARAGUS-POTATO SOUP

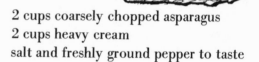

2 cups rich chicken stock
1 large potato, peeled and diced
5 green onions, chopped

2 cups coarsely chopped asparagus
2 cups heavy cream
salt and freshly ground pepper to taste

Combine the chicken stock, potato and green onions in a saucepan and simmer until potato is very soft. Add the asparagus and cook until al dente. With a wire whisk, gradually beat the cream into the soup. Season with salt and pepper and heat thoroughly; do not boil.
Serves 6

Note This soup may also be chilled and served cold.

ASPARAGUS-SOLE SOUP

2 cups rich chicken stock
1 cup asparagus purée
6 to 8 ounces filet of sole, cut
    into bite-size pieces

salt and freshly ground pepper
lemon wedges
minced dill for garnish

In a saucepan bring to a simmer the chicken stock and asparagus purée. Add the sole and simmer until fish is opaque and flakes easily with a fork. Season with salt and pepper to taste. Serve hot with lemon wedges and a garnish of minced dill.
Serves 3 or 4

CURRY-ASPARAGUS SOUP

1 cup chopped cooked asparagus
3 cups rich chicken or turkey stock
3/4 teaspoon curry powder
1/4 teaspoon salt

1/8 teaspoon white pepper
minced dill
4 teaspoons sour cream

Purée in a blender or food processor the asparagus, 1 cup of the stock, curry powder, salt and white pepper. Combine asparagus mixture with the remaining 2 cups stock in a saucepan over medium heat and heat until near boiling. Serve with a garnish of minced dill on a teaspoon of sour cream.
Serves 4

Variation Proceed as directed adding only 1 cup of stock to the saucepan. Remove from heat and stir in 1 cup of heavy cream. Chill and serve cold.

41

salads & snacks

RAW ASPARAGUS

A variety of sauces, hot and cold, may be served with raw asparagus for dipping. Garlic Cheese Sauce, page 30, and Fresh Avocado Dip, page 32, are both good choices. You may wish to arrange a platter of raw vegetables that includes not only asparagus but others as well: cherry tomatoes, cucumber sticks, mushrooms, cauliflowerets, broccoli flowerets, zucchini, snow peas, kohlrabi, fennel, etc. Breadsticks make a nice addition.

MARINATED RAW ASPARAGUS SALAD

Marinade
1/2 cup olive oil
3 tablespoons cider vinegar or
    fresh lemon juice
1/2 teaspoon minced garlic
1/8 teaspoon crushed dried oregano
    or marjoram

2 asparagus stalks, grated or
    thinly sliced
6 mushrooms, thinly sliced
1 cup snow peas
1 head Romaine lettuce, torn in bite-
    size pieces
sliced cherry tomatoes and alfalfa
    sprouts for garnish

Combine marinade ingredients and blend well. Place the asparagus, mushrooms and snow peas in marinade and refrigerate overnight. In a large salad bowl toss the Romaine lettuce with the marinade and vegetables. Serve garnished with tomatoes and sprouts.
Serves 4

ASPARAGUS VINAIGRETTE

1 pound asparagus, steamed al dente
   and kept hot
3/4 cup walnut oil or safflower oil
1/4 cup cider vinegar or fresh lemon
   juice

1 shallot, finely minced
salt and freshly ground pepper to taste
minced chives, parsley or dill
   for garnish

Arrange the asparagus in a shallow dish with the tips all in one direction. Combine walnut oil, vinegar, shallot and salt and pepper and pour over warm asparagus. Lift stalks so that all are coated with the dressing. Cool, then refrigerate for several hours. Thirty minutes before serving remove from the refrigerator. Just before serving garnish with minced chives, parsley or dill.
Serves 4

Dressing Variations
- Substitute white wine vinegar for the cider vinegar.
- Add prepared German- or French-style mustard to taste.

PICKLED ASPARAGUS

1/2 cup cider vinegar
1/2 cup red wine
4 green onions, chopped
4 peppercorns

1/2 teaspoon dill seed
1/4 teaspoon salt
1 pound asparagus, steamed al dente
   and kept hot

Heat together the vinegar, wine, onions, peppercorns, dill seed and salt until hot. Pour over asparagus, let cool, cover and refrigerate for 2 days before serving.
Serves 4

GREEN SALAD

For each serving
1 artichoke bottom, cooked
1/4 cup each cut-up cooked asparagus
    tips (1-inch lengths) and avocado
    cubes

2 tablespoons Garlic Cheese Sauce,
    page 30
minced parsley or dill and lemon
    wedges for garnish

Place the artichoke bottom on a salad plate. Combine the asparagus tips and avocado cubes with enough sauce to coat the vegetables well, toss lightly and spoon onto the artichokes. Garnish with parsley or dill and lemon wedges.

HOT AND SPICY SALAD

4 slices bacon, cut into 1-inch pieces
1 cup coarsely chopped asparagus
1-1/2 to 2 tablespoons Hot Stuff,
    page 32

1 tablespoon cider vinegar
1/2 head leaf lettuce, torn in bite-
    size pieces

In a skillet sauté the bacon until crisp. Remove bacon from pan, reserving drippings, and crumble when cool; set aside. Sauté the asparagus in 4 tablespoons of the reserved drippings until al dente. Mix in Hot Stuff, vinegar and reserved bacon. Remove from the heat, toss the lettuce in the skillet and serve immediately.
Serves 4

Note If the skillet is not large enough to easily toss the lettuce, pour the asparagus mixture into a large salad bowl and toss the leaves through the mixture quickly, allowing extra liquid to remain at the bottom of the bowl. You can also prepare and serve this salad in a wok.

"HOT AND SOUR" COLD ASPARAGUS

1-1/2 pounds asparagus, steamed
   al dente, cut into 2-inch lengths
   and kept hot
grated zest of 1 orange
6 tablespoons corn oil

2 tablespoons cider vinegar
2 tablespoons Hot Stuff, page 32
1/4 teaspoon dry mustard

Toss asparagus with zest of orange. Combine remaining ingredients and pour over asparagus; toss lightly. Place asparagus in the refrigerator to marinate for 24 hours before serving; stir several times during this period. Remove from refrigerator 1 hour before serving to bring to room temperature.
Serves 4

TAMARI SALAD

2 cups cut-up cooked asparagus
   (1-inch lengths)
1 medium avocado, cubed
alfalfa sprouts and/or sliced
   cherry tomatoes

2 tablespoons tamari soy sauce
1 tablespoon fresh lemon juice

Place 1/2 cup asparagus and 1/4 cup avocado cubes in each of 4 individual salad bowls. Garnish each salad with alfalfa sprouts and/or tomato slices. Mix together the tamari soy sauce and lemon juice and sprinkle a little over each salad. This dressing is strong-flavored, so only a small amount is necessary.
Serves 4

ASPARAGUS AND WALNUT SALAD

1 cup walnut halves
1/3 cup tamari soy sauce
1/3 cup sugar
1/3 cup cider vinegar

3 tablespoons walnut oil or safflower oil
1-1/2 pounds asparagus, steamed al
    dente, cut into 1-inch pieces and
    kept hot

Roast the walnuts in a preheated 300° oven 20 minutes; chop coarsely and set aside. In a saucepan combine tamari soy sauce, sugar, vinegar and oil and place over low heat, stirring until sugar dissolves. Remove from heat and mix walnuts into dressing. Pour dressing over asparagus and toss lightly; chill. Remove salad from refrigerator 30 minutes before serving.
Serves 4

ASPARAGUS IN AVOCADO BOATS

2 large avocados, halved, pulp
    removed and skins reserved
1/2 cup Hollandaise Sauce, page 26, or
1/2 cup Blender Mayonnaise,
    page 30

juice of half a lemon or to taste
3 cups cold cooked asparagus tips,
    cut into 1-inch pieces
lemon wedges for garnish

Purée avocado pulp in a blender or food processor. In a mixing bowl fold together the avocado pulp, Hollandaise Sauce, lemon juice and asparagus tips. Fill the 4 avocado skins with this mixture. Serve chilled garnished with lemon wedges.
Serves 4

GRILLED ASPARAGUS AND CHEESE ON TOAST

Mix butter with prepared horseradish to taste and spread on thin slices of dark bread, such as pumpernickel. Cover bread slices with a single layer of cooked asparagus stalks or asparagus purée and sprinkle generously with grated Swiss cheese. Place under a preheated broiler until cheese browns and bubbles. Cut into diagonal halves to serve.

ASPARAGUS AND HAM ROLLS

Spread thin slices of boiled ham or prosciutto with softened cream cheese. Wrap ham slices around cooked and chilled asparagus tips. Secure with a toothpick.

Variations
- Add fresh lemon juice and ground walnuts to cream cheese.
- Mix asparagus purée with the cream cheese and roll ham slices without the asparagus tips.

ASPARAGUS ON NUT TOAST

homemade nut or fruit bread   Hollandaise Sauce, page 26
hot, freshly cooked asparagus stalks

For each person to be served, toast 1 slice of nut or fruit bread and place on a large serving plate. On each slice of toast arrange 4 to 6 asparagus stalks. Cover each serving with a large spoonful of warm Hollandaise Sauce and serve immediately.

Note The bread may be wrapped in foil and heated in the oven rather than toasted.

ASPARAGUS NUT SPREAD

8 ounces cream cheese, at room
   temperature

1/4 cup asparagus purée
2 tablespoons finely ground pecans

Cream the cream cheese until it is smooth and soft. Add the asparagus purée and pecans and mix well. Serve on crackers or freshly made toast.

ASPARAGUS CHEESE POCKETS

8 ounces cream cheese, at room
   temperature
8 ounces feta cheese, crumbled
2 eggs, beaten

1-1/3 cups asparagus purée
30 phyllo leaves (1-1/4 to 1-1/2
   pounds)
1 pound sweet butter, melted

Mix cheeses, eggs and asparagus purée together and refrigerate for 1 hour. Place 1 phyllo leaf on a flat surface and brush thoroughly with melted butter, including edges. Then stack 2 more leaves on top, brushing each with butter. With a sharp knife cut the stack of leaves into 4 lengthwise strips. Place 1 teaspoonful of the cheese mixture at the end of one strip and fold over 1 corner of the strip to make a triangular pocket, then continue to fold over in triangles to the end of the strip. Brush the pocket with melted butter and repeat the procedure with the remaining strips of phyllo leaves. Repeat with the remaining phyllo leaves and filling and bake in a preheated 500° oven for 20 minutes or until brown. These pockets may be made several hours ahead. Place them on cookie sheets, cover and store in the refrigerator. Makes 40 pockets

hot side dishes

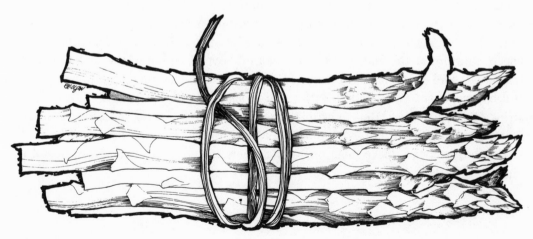

Steam 1 pound of asparagus until al dente. Arrange on a warmed serving dish with the tips all in one direction. Serve hot with any one of the following suggestions, adding salt to taste, if desired.
Serves 2 or 3

- 1/4 pound butter, melted, and freshly ground pepper to taste
- 1/4 pound butter, melted, and freshly ground pepper and fresh lemon juice to taste
- 1/4 pound butter, melted, and 1 tablespoon finely grated unsalted nutmeats
- 1/4 pound butter, melted, 3 tablespoons fresh lemon juice and 2 tablespoons capers
- Dill Butter: Cream together 1/4 pound butter and 1 tablespoon minced dill.
- Curry Butter: Cream together 1/4 pound butter and 1 teaspoon curry powder, or to taste.
- Garlic Butter: Cream together 1/4 pound butter and 1 teaspoon garlic powder or 2 garlic cloves, minced.
- Lemon Butter: Cream together 1/4 pound butter and the grated zest of half a lemon.
- Orange Butter: Cream together 1/4 pound butter and the grated zest of half an orange.
- Blender Mayonnaise, page 30
- Garlic Mayonnaise, page 30
- Horseradish Mayonnaise: Mix 1 teaspoon prepared horseradish into 1 cup mayonnaise.
- Mustard Mayonnaise: Mix 1 teaspoon Dijon-style mustard into 1 cup mayonnaise.
- Mousseline Sauce, page 27

Serving suggestions continued on following page

- Béchamel Sauce, page 28
- Hollandaise Sauce, page 26
- Hollandaise Sauce with additional fresh lemon juice and grated zest to taste
- Hollandaise Sauce with fresh orange juice and grated zest to taste
- Rice Sauce, page 29
- Mornay Sauce, page 28
- Celery Sauce, page 31
- Whipped cream with fresh orange juice and grated zest to taste
- Whipped cream with fresh lemon juice and grated zest to taste
- 1/4 cup heavy cream, whipped, folded into 1 cup mayonnaise
- 1 cup sour cream whipped with 3 tablespoons fresh orange juice
- 1 cup sour cream whipped with 2 tablespoons prepared horseradish; let stand 2 hours before serving.
- Fresh Avocado Dip, page 32
- Garlic Cheese Sauce, page 30
- Hot applesauce
- Mix 1 tablespoon fresh lemon juice with 3 tablespoons olive oil; add chopped chives, dill or green onion, if desired.
- Sieve 2 hard-cooked eggs over asparagus; then sprinkle with a mixture of 1 tablespoon fresh lemon juice and 3 tablespoons olive oil.
- Sprinkle with toasted sesame seeds and tamari soy sauce.

ASPARAGUS BROIL

Place a single layer of cooked asparagus stalks in a shallow ovenproof dish. Sprinkle with salt and freshly ground pepper. Cover asparagus with a layer of thinly sliced peeled tomatoes. Lightly sprinkle over the top fresh bread crumbs, drizzle with brown butter and top with grated Parmesan cheese. Place the dish under a preheated broiler until hot and cheese has melted.

FOILED ASPARAGUS

1 pound asparagus
salt and freshly ground pepper

1 tablespoon butter
1/4 to 1/2 cup rich chicken stock

Place asparagus on a large sheet of aluminum foil with the edges folded to form a slight rim. Sprinkle asparagus with salt and pepper, dot with butter and carefully pour stock over. Then fold sides of foil over the asparagus to form a sealed cooking container. Place on a baking sheet and bake in a preheated 400° oven for 20 to 30 minutes, or until asparagus is al dente. Lift asparagus from foil, place on a warmed serving dish and pour cooking juices over the top. Serve immediately.
Serves 4

Variations Add tomato slices, chopped green onions, green apple slices or fresh pineapple chunks to the asparagus before cooking.

WRAPPED ASPARAGUS

cooked asparagus stalks
thin slices of prosciutto or boiled ham

grated Parmesan cheese
melted butter

Place 2 slender or 1 large asparagus stalk on each slice of prosciutto or ham, roll up and arrange in a single layer in an ovenproof dish. Sprinkle lightly with Parmesan cheese and drizzle with melted butter. Place in a 425° oven until the cheese bubbles (about 5 minutes).

Variation Omit meat and arrange the asparagus stalks in an ovenproof dish in a single layer. Proceed as directed in recipe.

ASPARAGUS-STUFFED MUSHROOMS

large mushrooms, with stems removed
melted butter
2 or 3 cooked asparagus tips for each
    mushroom

Blender Hollandaise Sauce, page 26
fresh lemon juice

Place the mushrooms in a shallow baking pan. Brush with melted butter and place under a preheated broiler. Broil 3 minutes on each side, basting with melted butter frequently. Drain excess butter from the mushroom caps and place 2 or 3 asparagus tips in each cap. Fill caps with 1 to 2 tablespoons hollandaise and broil for 3 to 5 minutes, until bubbly. Sprinkle mushrooms with lemon juice and serve hot.

ASPARAGUS SOUFFLÉ

2 tablespoons butter
2 shallots, minced
2 tablespoons flour
1/2 cup milk, heated
2 eggs, separated

2 cups asparagus purée
1/2 cup sour cream
1/2 cup grated Parmesan cheese
1/4 teaspoon salt
1/8 teaspoon white pepper

Heat the butter in a saucepan and sauté the shallots until translucent. Sprinkle the flour into the pan and cook and stir for 1 to 2 minutes; do not brown. Stir in the milk, then add the egg yolks, blending in well. Cook and stir over low heat until thickened. Remove from the heat; add the asparagus purée, sour cream, Parmesan cheese, and salt and pepper, mixing well. Beat the egg whites until stiff but not dry and fold into soufflé mixture. Put in a buttered 10-inch baking dish and bake in a preheated 375° oven for 45 minutes. This may be served with Celery Sauce.
Serves 6

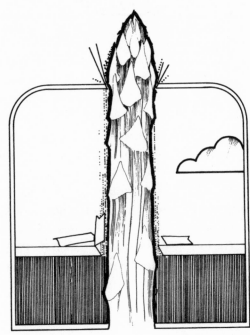

BROWN SUGAR ASPARAGUS

4 tablespoons butter

1 tablespoon brown sugar

2 cups cut-up asparagus (1-inch lengths)

1 to 1-1/2 cups rich chicken stock

Melt the butter in a skillet, add the sugar and stir until sugar is dissolved. Add asparagus and sauté 2 minutes; be careful it does not burn. Add the chicken stock, cover and cook over medium-low heat 3 minutes. Cook uncovered for 2 minutes to reduce sauce. Serve hot in a warmed serving dish.

Serves 3 or 4

3 phyllo leaves
melted butter

12 large asparagus tips
freshly ground pepper

Place 1 phyllo leaf on a flat surface and brush thoroughly with melted butter, including edges. Stack the remaining 2 leaves on top, brushing each with butter. With a sharp pointed knife cut the stack of leaves in half lengthwise. Place 6 asparagus tips on one end of a strip and grind pepper over them. Fold over one corner of the strip to make a triangle shape. Continue folding from side to side, as you would a flag, ending with a triangular-shaped packet. Brush top with melted butter and place on a lightly buttered baking sheet. Repeat with remaining phyllo and asparagus. Bake in a preheated 400° oven 20 minutes. Serve with melted butter or Garlic Cheese Sauce, if desired. Packets will stay hot for several minutes after removing from the oven.
Serves 2

Variations
- Sprinkle any kind of grated cheese over asparagus before folding phyllo.
- Mix fresh crab meat with enough mayonnaise to just moisten and spread over asparagus before folding phyllo.
- Place tomato slices on asparagus before folding phyllo.

Note Triangles may be made ahead and refrigerated until baking.

BAKED APPLES WITH ASPARAGUS

6 large cooking apples, cored to make
  large cavities

rich meat stock
18 or 24 asparagus stalks

Place the apples upright in a baking dish. Pour meat stock into the dish to a depth of
1/2 inch. Bake in a preheated 350° oven 45 minutes. Ten minutes before the end of
the cooking period, insert 3 or 4 asparagus stalks into the center of each apple so the
tips show over the top and baste the asparagus and apples with additional meat
stock. Place a sheet of foil over the apples to keep the asparagus tips moist. Return
apples to the oven and cook 5 to 7 minutes longer, making sure asparagus doesn't
overcook. Serve immediately as a side dish with roast lamb or pork.
Serves 6

SQUASH AND ASPARAGUS BAKE

2 Danish (acorn) squash
2 cups cut-up asparagus (1/2-inch
  lengths)

1/4 cup brown sugar
2 tablespoons rum or sherry
3 tablespoons butter, melted

Select the roundest squash available (this indicates a deep seed cavity). Cut in half
lengthwise and remove seeds and fibers. Place squash halves skin side up in a shallow
baking pan with water to a depth of 1/2 inch. Bake in a preheated 350° oven 45
minutes. Remove squash from the oven, combine remaining ingredients and spoon
into squash cavities. Check water level in pan and add water, if necessary, to
maintain 1/2-inch depth. Cover pan with aluminum foil, return to oven and bake for
7 to 10 minutes, or until asparagus is al dente. Serve immediately.
Serves 4

ASPARAGUS AND CORN SPOON BREAD

4 tablespoons butter, at room
   temperature
1 egg
1/2 cup heavy cream
1/2 cup freshly grated corn kernels
1/2 cup small curd cottage cheese
2 tablespoons sugar

1/2 teaspoon salt
3/4 cup unbleached flour
1-1/2 teaspoons baking powder
1/2 cup cornmeal
2 cups asparagus purée
1/4 pound Monterey jack cheese,
   thinly sliced

Cream together the butter, egg, cream, corn kernels and cottage cheese. Sift together the sugar, salt, flour and baking powder, mix in cornmeal and add to the creamed mixture, mixing well. Place half of this mixture in a buttered 10-inch baking dish. Spread the asparagus purée evenly over the top and cover purée with cheese slices. Spread remaining half of cornmeal mixture over top and bake in a preheated 425° oven for 45 minutes, or until well browned.
Serves 6

BAKED ASPARAGUS

1 cup fresh bread crumbs
3 small green onions, diced
4 tablespoons butter or corn oil
1/2 teaspoon salt
freshly ground pepper to taste

2 cups milk, heated
3 eggs, well beaten
4 cups coarsely chopped asparagus or
   asparagus purée

Sauté bread crumbs and green onions in butter or oil until crumbs are golden and onions are translucent. Season with salt and pepper and remove from heat; set aside. Slowly add the heated milk to the beaten eggs, stirring constantly. Combine egg mixture with sauté mixture and asparagus. Pour into a greased 1-1/2-quart baking-serving dish. Bake in a preheated 350° oven for 30 minutes or until custard is puffed and firm. Serve with Garlic Cheese Sauce, if desired.
Serves 6

Variation For a main course, double recipe and add 1 to 2 cups chopped cooked turkey, chicken or lamb when combining all ingredients.

ASPARAGUS PATTIES

2 pounds asparagus, grated or thinly
   sliced
2 eggs, lightly beaten
2 tablespoons unbleached flour

1/2 teaspoon salt
1/4 teaspoon freshly ground pepper
corn oil as needed

Mix together the asparagus, eggs, flour, salt and pepper. Heat 2 tablespoons corn oil in a skillet over medium heat. For each patty pour 1/4 cup of the asparagus mixture into the skillet and flatten slightly with a spatula. Cook 2 to 3 minutes until patty starts to brown; turn over and cook for 2 minutes. Repeat with remaining batter, adding oil to the pan as needed. Keep patties in foil in a warm oven until all are cooked. Serve with Mornay Sauce, if desired.
Serves 8

Variation Substitute 1 large potato, grated, for 1 pound of the asparagus. The asparagus should be grated, not sliced.

main dishes

SOFT SCRAMBLE WITH ASPARAGUS

4 eggs, well beaten
1/4 cup heavy cream
1 cup chopped cooked asparagus

salt and freshly ground pepper to taste
freshly made toast triangles or
toasted English muffins

Heat eggs and cream in the top of a double boiler over simmering water and cook and stir until mixture begins to thicken. While eggs are still liquid add the asparagus and cook and stir until eggs are set but still moist. Season with salt and pepper and serve over toast triangles or toasted English muffins with sliced smoked salmon, if desired.

Serves 2

ASPARAGUS OMELET

2 eggs
1 tablespoon asparagus purée
1/8 teaspoon salt

dash freshly ground pepper
1-1/2 teaspoons corn oil
1 tablespoon grated Parmesan cheese

Beat together the eggs, asparagus purée and salt and pepper. Heat the corn oil in an omelet pan until it is very hot and oil starts to smoke. Pour in the egg mixture and swirl it around until the mixture coats the pan bottom. Keeping the pan in motion over the heat by moving it back and forth quickly, lift the egg mixture with a knife edge or a spoon so uncooked portion flows underneath to cook. Remove the pan from the heat while the eggs are still moist on the surface. The cooking process should take 1 minute or less. Place the Parmesan cheese on half of the omelet, fold the omelet in half and slide it onto a warm plate. Serve immediately.

Serves 1

ASPARAGUS PICNIC PIE

Pie Crust dough, page 33
1-1/2 cups heavy cream
3 eggs
1 jalapeno chili pepper (fresh or
   canned), seeded and liquified in
   a blender or food processor

2 cups chopped cooked asparagus
1 cup grated Parmesan, Swiss or
   Jarlsberg cheese
1/2 teaspoon salt

Line a 12-inch pizza pan with pie crust dough. Combine the cream and eggs and beat well. Add pepper, asparagus, cheese and salt; mix well. Fill the pizza pan with mixture and bake in a preheated 350° oven for 25 to 30 minutes, or until custard is puffed and firm. Remove from oven and let cool. Serve at room temperature, cut in wedges, accompanied with cold beer. Refrigerate any leftover pie.
Serves 6

ASPARAGUS QUICK CRUST PIE

egg bread or whole wheat bread slices
1/2 cup crumbled cooked bacon or
   chopped boiled ham
2 cups heavy cream

3 eggs
1/2 cup grated Parmesan, Swiss or
   Jarlsberg cheese
1 cup chopped cooked asparagus

Line the bottom of a 10- or 12-inch pie dish with bread slices. Sprinkle the bacon over them. Combine the cream, eggs, cheese and asparagus and mix until blended. Pour over bread and bake in a preheated 350° oven for 30 to 40 minutes or until the custard is puffed and firm. Serve hot or at room temperature for lunch or dinner.
Serves 6

4 ounces cream cheese
1/4 cup cottage cheese
1/4 cup crumbled feta cheese
2 eggs, lightly beaten
2 tablespoons farina
1/2 to 1 pound asparagus, cooked and
coarsely chopped or puréed

1 teaspoon salt
1/4 teaspoon freshly ground pepper
about 1 pound phyllo leaves, at room
temperature and kept covered to
prevent them from drying out
1 pound butter, melted

Combine cream cheese, cottage cheese, feta, eggs, farina, asparagus, and salt and
pepper in a large bowl and mix well; set aside. Line a deep 10-inch cooking-serving
container with 8 phyllo leaves, brushing each one, including the edges, with butter as
it is placed in the dish. Pour in half of the asparagus mixture. Place 4 phyllo leaves
over filling, brushing each one with butter as it is placed in the dish. Pour in
remaining filling and cover with 8 more phyllo leaves, again buttering each one as it
is placed in the dish. Fold the edges of the bottom layers of phyllo over the top
layers of phyllo. Brush the top with butter thoroughly. Lightly sprinkle the top with
water and with a sharp knife point cut a few vents in the top layer of leaves. Bake in
a preheated 350° oven for 40 minutes. Serve hot or cold.
Serves 6 to 8

Variation Substitute 1 cup chopped cooked meat or seafood for 1 cup of the
asparagus.

SPRING PIZZA

2 cups Natural Tomato Sauce, page 31
1/4 cup chopped prosciutto
1-1/2 to 2 cups coarsely chopped
  asparagus or asparagus purée

Pizza Dough, following
1/4 cup grated Romano cheese
1 cup loosely packed grated
  mozzarella cheese

Combine the tomato sauce and prosciutto in a saucepan and cook over low heat for 1 hour. Mix in asparagus and set aside. Press pizza dough into pan as directed in dough recipe. Spoon sauce onto dough and sprinkle cheeses over the top. Bake in a preheated 500° oven for 15 minutes.
Serves 4 to 6

PIZZA DOUGH

1 tablespoon active dry yeast
  (1 package)
1 cup lukewarm water (110° to 115°)

1 teaspoon salt
3-1/2 cups unbleached flour
1 tablespoon butter, melted

Dissolve the yeast in the water and let yeast mixture stand for a few minutes, until the yeast bubbles up. Combine the salt and flour in a large mixing bowl and make a well in the center. Pour the yeast mixture and the melted butter into the well and mix the dough with your fingertips or a fork until it forms a rough ball. Turn the dough out onto a lightly floured board and knead 10 minutes, or until the dough is smooth and elastic. Place the dough in a lightly oiled bowl, cover with a tea towel and place in a warm, draft-free spot. Let the dough rise until double in bulk, about 1-1/2 to 2 hours. Then remove the dough from the bowl and knead for 1 minute. With fingertips, press the dough into an oiled 12-inch pizza pan.

1 unbaked 10-inch Pie Crust,
  page 33
3 eggs
2 cups heavy cream

3/4 cup grated Parmesan or Swiss cheese
1/8 teaspoon freshly ground pepper
dash ground nutmeg
1 cup asparagus purée

Prepare the pie crust and set aside. In a mixing bowl beat the eggs, cream, cheese, pepper and nutmeg until well blended. Add the asparagus purée and mix in thoroughly. Pour mixture into the pie crust and bake for 35 to 45 minutes, or until the center is firm and puffed. Serve hot or cold.
Serves 6 to 8

Variations
• Before baking make a spoked wheel design of asparagus stalks on the top of the quiche.
• Add 1 cup chopped cooked ham, chicken, turkey or seafood with the asparagus purée.
• Bake the filling in a pie dish without the crust.

ASPARAGUS AND OYSTER BROIL

1 pound asparagus, steamed al dente
24 fresh small oysters, shucked
2 cups Blender Hollandaise Sauce,
    page 26

1/4 cup fresh lemon juice
minced parsley for garnish
French bread as accompaniment

Place the asparagus in a single layer in a large shallow baking dish. Top with oysters. Combine the Hollandaise Sauce and lemon juice and pour over the asparagus and oysters. Place under a preheated broiler for 7 to 10 minutes. Garnish with minced parsley and serve hot with French bread.

Serves 2 as an entrée; 4 to 6 as a first course

OYSTERS IN SPRINGTIME

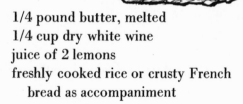

24 fresh small oysters, shucked
freshly ground pepper
2 cups asparagus purée
1 tablespoon minced tarragon
1/2 teaspoon salt

1/4 pound butter, melted
1/4 cup dry white wine
juice of 2 lemons
freshly cooked rice or crusty French
    bread as accompaniment

Place oysters in a single layer in a buttered shallow baking dish. Grind pepper lightly over oysters; then spoon over asparagus purée and sprinkle with tarragon and salt. Combine butter, wine and lemon juice and pour over purée. Place under a preheated broiler for 15 minutes or until dish is bubbly. Oysters will be opaque when cooked. Serve with rice or French bread.
Serves 2

SHRIMP AND ASPARAGUS FETTUCCINE

1/2 cup heavy cream
1/2 cup milk
1 cup grated white cheese
   (Gruyère or Jarlsberg)
1 cup grated Parmesan cheese
4 egg yolks

1 pound cooked fresh shrimp
1 pound asparagus tips, cooked
dash ground nutmeg
freshly ground pepper to taste
Dill or Asparagus Noodles, page 34, 35
lemon slices for garnish

Combine the cream, milk and cheeses in the top of a double boiler placed over simmering water. Cook and stir until cheeses melt; do not boil. Beat in the egg yolks, one at a time. Cook and stir until sauce thickens. Then add the shrimp, asparagus tips, nutmeg and pepper. Serve over noodles and garnish with lemon slices.
Serves 4

ASPARAGUS AND SALMON CRÊPE CAKE

Crêpes
1/2 cup water
1/4 cup heavy cream
1/4 cup milk
3 eggs
1 cup unbleached flour
1-1/2 tablespoons butter, melted
corn oil for cooking

Filling
8 ounces cream cheese
2 cups flaked cooked salmon
2 cups puréed asparagus

double recipe of Mornay Sauce,
    page 28

To make the crêpes combine all the ingredients except corn oil and beat until smooth. Refrigerate for at least 3 hours before cooking. Lightly oil a 7-inch crêpe pan by rubbing with oiled paper toweling. Place the pan over medium-high heat until the oil starts to smoke slightly. Pour in 1/4 cup of the batter and tip the pan so the batter evenly covers the bottom. When the underside of the crêpe is brown, lift with both hands, using index fingers and thumbs, and turn over to brown top side. Remove the crêpe from the pan and place on a plate. Repeat with remaining batter, stacking crêpes as you go and keeping them covered. After each crêpe is made use the original oiled paper toweling to wipe the pan before adding batter for the next crêpe. You should have 10 crêpes when all of the batter has been used. The crêpes may be prepared ahead, well wrapped and stored in the refrigerator until you are ready to make the cake.

To make the filling combine the cream cheese, salmon and asparagus and blend well. Begin assembling the cake by placing 1 crêpe on the bottom of a baking dish. Spread with about 1/2 cup of the filling and top with a crêpe. Continue stacking the crêpes and filling in this manner, ending with a crêpe. You will now have a 10-layer cake. Pour Mornay Sauce over cake. Bake in a preheated 375° oven 30 minutes.
Serves 8

69

ASPARAGUS AND FISH MOUSSE

1 pound filet of sole
4 eggs, separated
1 cup milk
2 cups grated or chopped asparagus
3 tablespoons farina

1/2 teaspoon salt
1/4 teaspoon white pepper
1 cup heavy cream
1/4 cup fresh bread crumbs or cracker
    crumbs

Purée or chop the sole in a blender or food processor. Combine sole with the egg yolks, milk, asparagus, farina and salt and pepper, and mix until well blended. Whip the egg whites until stiff but not dry. Whip the cream until stiff and gently combine with the egg whites. Fold this mixture into the fish mixture and pour into an oiled 6-cup mold lined with bread or cracker crumbs. Cover mold with aluminum foil and place in a pan of hot water to a depth of two-thirds that of the mold. Bake in a preheated 350° oven for 1 hour and 15 minutes. Invert on a serving platter to unmold. Serve hot or cold with Curry Mayonnaise or Celery Sauce, if desired. Serves 6

SALMON-ASPARAGUS LOAF

2 eggs, beaten
1 16-ounce can salmon with liquid (or
    equal amount of cooked fish with
    clam juice as juice)
1 cup fresh bread crumbs
1 cup chopped cooked asparagus

1 tablespoon curry powder
1/4 teaspoon salt
1/8 teaspoon freshly ground pepper
Natural Tomato Sauce, page 31,
    seasoned with salt and pepper

Combine all ingredients except tomato sauce in a large bowl, mixing well. Pour into a 1-1/2- or 2-quart casserole and bake in a preheated 350° oven for 30 to 40 minutes or until firm. Serve with Natural Tomato Sauce.
Serves 4

Variation Substitute diced cooked chicken for the salmon and chicken broth for the liquid.

ASPARAGUS BAKED IN SALMON

1 10-pound whole fresh salmon	1-1/2 to 2 pounds asparagus
salt	freshly ground pepper
1 medium onion, thinly sliced	melted butter with minced dill
2 lemons, thinly sliced	2 lemons, cut into wedges

Place the salmon on a large sheet of aluminum foil. Salt the cavity and fill with the onion and lemon slices. Seal the foil around the fish and bake in a preheated 325° oven for 30 to 40 minutes, or until flesh at the thickest part of the fish begins to turn opaque. Remove from the oven, discard onion and lemon slices and fill salmon cavity with asparagus. Reseal foil around the fish and return to the oven for 10 minutes or until asparagus is al dente. Serve fish and asparagus on a warmed platter with freshly ground pepper and melted butter with dill on top and lemon wedges on the side.
Serves 8 to 10

Variation Eight to 10 fresh trout may be substituted for the salmon.

CHICKEN AND ASPARAGUS

slices of cooked chicken or turkey
  breast meat
lightly buttered slices of freshly
  toasted French bread or egg bread
cooked asparagus stalks

melted butter
slices of Emmenthaler or Jarlsberg
  cheese
slices of fresh pineapple for
  accompaniment

For each serving arrange slices of chicken or turkey on slices of freshly toasted bread on a greased baking sheet. Place 2 or 3 asparagus stalks on top of each portion, and sprinkle each with 1 teaspoon of melted butter. Top each portion with a slice of cheese and place under a preheated broiler for 5 minutes or until cheese is bubbling and brown. Serve hot accompanied with pineapple slices.

ASPARAGUS AND TURKEY CASSEROLE

Sauce
3/4 cup Blender Mayonnaise,
  page 30
1/2 cup Blender Hollandaise Sauce,
  page 26
1-1/2 cups half-and-half cream
2 cups coarsely chopped cooked
  asparagus

Blender Mayonnaise for coating
1/4 pound Curry Noodles, page 35,
  cooked
3 cups chopped cooked turkey or
  chicken
1-1/2 cups grated Parmesan cheese

Combine the sauce ingredients and mix together until smooth; set aside. Spread a thin coating of mayonnaise on the bottom of an ovenproof 2-quart casserole. Then place one-third of the noodles in the dish. Cover the noodles with half of the turkey, pour on one-third of the sauce and sprinkle with half of the cheese. Repeat layering and top with the last third of the noodles and sauce. Place in a preheated 350° oven for 35 to 45 minutes or until bubbly.

Serves 6

CURRIED ASPARAGUS AND CHICKEN LIVERS

1/2 cup chopped onion

1 pound chicken livers, lightly coated
  with flour

1 pound asparagus, cut into 1-inch
  pieces

3 tablespoons corn oil

2 tablespoons dry white wine

2 teaspoons curry powder, mixed with

1 cup heavy cream

freshly cooked rice as accompaniment

Sauté onion, chicken livers and asparagus in corn oil until chicken livers lose their redness. Add the wine and cover and simmer until asparagus is al dente, about 3 to 5 minutes. Add curry powder-cream mixture to pan and cook, stirring constantly, until cream thickens. (Add more cream if the sauce is too thick.) Serve over freshly cooked rice.

Serves 4

A CROWN FOR ASPARAGUS

1 8-pound crown roast of pork
3 to 4 pounds asparagus, 6 to 8 inches
   in length

1 cup Hollandaise Sauce, page 26

Bake crown roast in a preheated 325° oven 3-1/2 to 4 hours (25 to 30 minutes per pound). Thirty minutes before the roast has finished cooking, place asparagus stalks in cavity. Cover stalks with foil and continue baking. Remove from the oven and pour Hollandaise Sauce over the asparagus. Carve the roast at the table.
Serves 8 to 10

Variation A crown roast of lamb may be substituted for the pork. Adjust roasting time accordingly.

SOY ASPARAGUS

1-1/2 pounds turkey or chicken breast
   meat, pork tenderloin, or seafood
   such as shrimp or scallops, cut into
   bite-size pieces
1 slice ginger root
6 green onions, chopped
3 to 4 tablespoons corn oil
2 tablespoons sugar

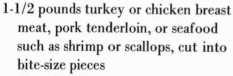

1/3 cup tamari soy sauce
3 cups water
1/2 pound or more asparagus, cut into
   1-inch lengths
2 tablespoons cornstarch, mixed with
2 tablespoons dry white wine
freshly cooked rice

Sauté the meat or seafood, ginger root and onions in corn oil until onions are translucent. Mix together the sugar, tamari soy sauce and water and add to the pan. Then add the asparagus and simmer for 8 to 10 minutes, stirring occasionally. Add cornstarch mixture and cook and stir until the sauce is thick and clear. Serve hot with steamed rice.

Serves 4

SWEET AND SOUR STIR-FRY

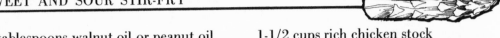

3 tablespoons walnut oil or peanut oil
1 slice ginger root
1 garlic clove, bruised
1 pound chicken breast meat, cut into
    bite-size pieces
1 pound asparagus, cut into 1/2-inch
    pieces on the diagonal

1-1/2 cups rich chicken stock
1/3 cup sugar
1/2 cup cider vinegar
2 tablespoons dry white wine
1 tablespoon cornstarch, mixed with
1-1/2 tablespoons sherry
freshly cooked rice

Heat oil in a skillet or wok and stir-fry ginger and garlic 10 seconds. Add chicken and asparagus and continue stir-frying until asparagus is just al dente and chicken juices run clear. Mix together chicken stock, sugar, vinegar and wine and add to skillet. Simmer about 3 minutes and add cornstarch mixture. Cook and stir until the sauce is thick and clear. Serve hot with steamed rice.

Serves 4

1 pound lean ground beef
1/4 cup wheat germ
1/2 cup heavy cream
1 egg
1/2 teaspoon crushed dried marjoram
1/2 teaspoon crushed dried oregano

1/2 teaspoon crushed dried thyme
dash ground nutmeg
1/2 teaspoon salt
1/4 teaspoon freshly ground pepper
6 to 8 asparagus stalks, cooked al dente
hot applesauce as accompaniment

Combine all ingredients except asparagus and hot applesauce and knead or grind to a pastelike consistency. Place half the meat mixture in a standard-size loaf pan. Place the asparagus stalks in the pan and press them firmly into the meat mixture. Press the remaining meat mixture into the pan and place in a preheated 350° oven for 1 hour. Slice and serve with hot applesauce.
Serves 4

peanut oil
1 garlic clove
meat and seafood platters:
  chicken or turkey breast meat, cut
    into 1-inch cubes
  prawns, shelled and deveined
  lamb, preferably from the leg, cut
    into 1-inch cubes
  filet of sole, cut into 1-inch pieces
vegetable platters:
  asparagus stalks
  snow peas
green beans
mushrooms
green onions
sweet potatoes, sliced
cauliflowerets
dipping sauces:
  tamari soy sauce with a side dish of
    toasted sesame seeds
  horseradish-flavored mayonnaise,
    sour cream or whipped cream
  Hollandaise Sauce, page 26
  melted butter

Fill a fondue pot two-thirds full with peanut oil, add garlic clove and heat oil until a cube of dry bread browns quickly when dropped into the oil. Place the fondue pot on a table heating unit that will keep the oil near the boiling temperature. Arrange the raw meats, seafood and vegetables on platters and place them around the fondue pot. Place the dipping sauces in bowls, from which the guests can spoon some of the sauces onto their own dinner plates. Provide each guest with at least 2 fondue forks, so that he can have two different things cooking at the same time. Each guest selects foods from the platters by spearing them with a fork and cooks them to desired doneness in the oil. Crusty French bread or rolls make a nice accompaniment.

Note Plan on about 1/3 pound each vegetables and meat or seafood for each person. If you do not have a fondue pot, an electric skillet may be used.

desserts

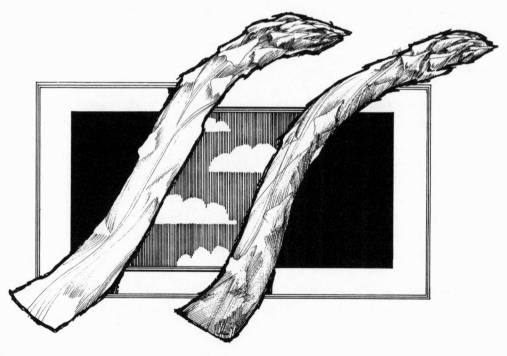

ASPARAGUS WHIP

1 cup finely chopped cooked asparagus
4 tablespoons sugar
1 tablespoon fresh lemon juice
1 tablespoon fresh orange juice
1/4 teaspoon salt
grated zest of 1/2 orange

1/2 teaspoon vanilla extract
2 tablespoons finely ground almonds or
  walnuts
3/4 cup heavy cream, whipped until
  stiff

In a blender purée the asparagus, 3 tablespoons of the sugar, lemon and orange juices, salt and orange zest. Add the remaining 1 tablespoon sugar, vanilla extract, and nuts to the whipped cream and fold whipped cream mixture into asparagus purée mixture. Chill for several hours and serve in demitasse cups.
Serves 6

ASPARAGUS SHERBET

1 quart milk
1-1/2 cups sugar
1-1/2 cups smooth asparagus purée
juice of 2 lemons

garnish of one of the following: finely
  ground walnuts, fresh or candied
  violets, borage flowers or thin slices
  of candied orange peel

Beat together the milk and sugar until sugar is dissolved. Place in freezer and freeze for 1 hour or until partially frozen. Spoon into a mixing bowl and add the asparagus purée and lemon juice. Beat well with an electric mixer, then return to freezer for 2 hours. Serve with garnish of choice as a dessert or to accompany roasted meats.
Makes 1-1/2 quarts

Note The sherbet becomes too hard if a rich milk or cream is used in this recipe.

ASPARAGUS ICE CREAM

4 cups milk
3/4 cup smooth asparagus purée
1 teaspoon vanilla extract

3/4 cup sugar
4 egg yolks

Mix together the milk, asparagus purée and vanilla and place over low heat. In another pan combine the sugar and egg yolks, place over low heat and beat with a whisk until the sugar dissolves. Slowly add, 1/2 cup at a time, the hot milk mixture to the egg mixture, stirring constantly. Stir until custard starts to thicken and coats the spoon. Remove from heat and let cool. Pour mixture into 2 cold ice-cube trays without dividers, cover with foil and freeze for 1-1/2 hours. Remove from trays and beat well. Return to trays and freeze for 30 minutes. Repeat beating and freeze for 30 minutes. Then beat a last time and freeze until ready to serve.
Makes 2 quarts

ASPARAGUS CHEESECAKE

Cheesecake
2 pounds ricotta cheese
2 cups smooth asparagus purée
6 eggs
2/3 cup sugar
1/4 cup unbleached flour
1/4 cup heavy cream

2 tablespoons grated orange zest
2 tablespoons vanilla extract
dash ground nutmeg

Mandarin Orange Sauce
1 11-ounce can mandarin orange
    segments, drained
1 tablespoon confectioners' sugar

Combine all ingredients for cheesecake and mix well. Pour into an oiled and floured 8-inch spring-form pan and bake in a preheated 375° oven for 50 to 60 minutes. Let cool before removing ring form.

To prepare the orange sauce purée the mandarin orange segments in a blender or food processor. Add the confectioners' sugar and blend in well. Serve the cheesecake at room temperature, or chilled, with sauce to pour over. This cake will also keep for several days refrigerated.

Serves 8

Variation Substitute orange-flavored whipped cream for the orange sauce.

ASPARAGUS AND NUT FRUIT CAKE

4 eggs
1/2 cup sugar
1 teaspoon vanilla extract
1 teaspoon salt

1/2 cup minced candied orange peel
1-1/2 cups unbleached flour
1 cup asparagus purée
1 cup chopped walnuts

Combine the eggs, sugar, vanilla extract and salt and mix until smooth. Blend the candied orange peel with the flour and add to the batter, mixing in thoroughly. Fold in the asparagus purée and chopped nuts, again mixing well. Pour batter into an oiled and floured standard-size loaf pan and bake in a preheated 325° oven for 50 to 60 minutes or until a knife inserted in the center comes out clean. Serve with butter while warm. Serve with cream cheese the following day.

Makes 1 cake

Custard
1/2 cup milk
1/4 teaspoon vanilla extract
1/4 cup smooth asparagus purée
6 tablespoons sugar
2 egg yolks

Puffs
1/2 cup water
4 tablespoons butter
1/2 cup unbleached flour
2 eggs

1/2 cup heavy cream

To make the custard mix together the milk, vanilla extract and asparagus purée and place over low heat. In another pan combine the sugar and egg yolks, place over low heat and beat with a whisk until the sugar dissolves. Slowly add, 1/4 cup at a time, the hot milk mixture to the egg mixture, stirring constantly. Stir until the custard starts to thicken and coats the spoon. Cool, cover and refrigerate.

To make the puffs combine the water and butter in a medium-size saucepan and bring to a boil. Remove from the heat and add the flour, beating until smooth. Beat the eggs, one at a time, into the batter until it shines. Drop 10 to 12 rounded tablespoons of the batter onto an oiled baking sheet and bake in a preheated 450° oven for 15 minutes. Lower oven temperature to 325° and bake 10 minutes more. Remove from the oven and allow puffs to cool for 2 hours before cutting them in half crosswise.

Whip the cream until stiff and fold into custard. Remove tops of puffs and fill with cream-custard mixture. Replace tops and serve freshly filled or chilled.
Makes 10 to 12 puffs; serves 5 or 6

Note The puffs may be made 2 or 3 days before you plan to serve them. Leave uncut and store in airtight plastic bags in the refrigerator.

ASPARAGUS-LEMON PIE

Crust
1/2 pound butter
1/3 cup sugar
1/4 teaspoon salt
2 egg yolks
1 teaspoon vanilla extract
2-1/4 cups unbleached flour

Filling
3 eggs, separated
1/2 cup sugar
1/4 cup fresh lemon juice
2 teaspoons grated lemon zest
1/2 teaspoon salt
2 cups smooth asparagus purée
1/3 cup sugar

To make crust cream together the butter, sugar and salt. Add the egg yolks, vanilla extract and flour and mix together well. Press dough into an 8-inch spring-form pan and line with aluminum foil buttered on the underside. Fill with dried beans or rice and bake in a preheated 350° oven for 20 minutes. Let cool, but do not remove ring from pan.

To make the filling combine the egg yolks, the 1/2 cup sugar, lemon juice, lemon zest and salt in the top of a double boiler and beat until well blended; then place over simmering water in the lower pan. Stirring constantly, cook until the custard thickens and coats a spoon. Remove from the heat and fold in asparagus purée. Beat the egg whites until stiff, adding the 1/3 cup sugar while beating. Then fold egg whites into filling. Fill cooled crust with filling and bake in a preheated 325° oven for 30 minutes. Let cool on a rack and remove ring form.

Serves 6 to 8

ornamental asparagus

Ornamental asparagus has been a mainstay of the indoor plant garden since the late 1800's. Though commonly called asparagus ferns, they are not true ferns. It is the fernlike appearance of their foliage that has created this misnomer. Like the edible *Asparagus officinalis,* they belong to the lily family, and their new growth looks like a slender version of the stalks we serve at the table. In tropical areas where these ornamentals are native, the slender stalks are eaten.

There are 150 varieties of *Asparagus* aside from the common edible one, but only six are readily available to house-plant enthusiasts. One of the most often seen is *A. asparagoides,* known as smilax, which is often used by florists for cut foliage in bouquets. It is a small-leaved vine, the leaves glossy and grass green in color. Variety *'Myrtifolius'* is a smaller, more graceful version, and is known as baby smilax.

A. densiflorus 'Myeri,' commonly called foxtail fern, has a fluffy look. The stalks form a cone shape with dense needlelike foliage. This is one of the slower-maturing varieties.

With puffs of bright green needles and a beautiful pine-tree look, *A. densiflorus* *'Myriocladus'* (sometimes referred to as *A. retrofractus*) is one of the largest asparagus ferns grown indoors. It is possible to stake this fern into an upright position to best reveal its slender shape. Commonly known as the ming fern, it holds good promise of white blossoms when mature.

The sickle-thorn asparagus *(A. falcatus)* gets its name from the curved leaves which cover the stems, helping this plant to climb along walls with vine-like ease. Indoors it has been known to reach 6 to 8 feet. *A. plumosus* (also known as *A. setaceus*), of which there are at least 12 varieties, is another favorite of florists. Its vining foliage looks much like the mature foliage of *Asparagus officinalis,* and this dense, dark-green feathery mass, though delicate in appearance, is very durable.

The most popular of all the ornamental asparagus, and the most rewarding for the beginning indoor gardener, is *A. densiflorus* 'Sprengeri.' The lacy, shiny, bright-green foliage can be the main attraction in any room. With filtered sun or good artificial light and soil kept moist, it will be very happy, but it will also survive admirably in less than optimum conditions. This ornamental's good humor in spite of occasional mistreatment is to be applauded. A friend once told me her Sprenger fern had not produced any new growth for two years. As we talked she mentioned that she routinely cut off the strange "spikes" that appeared from time to time. She had not allowed the spears of new growth to show their form before she took the clippers to them. My grandmother, on the other hand, cut back all the foliage every winter to let the fern rest and rejuvenate itself. Then in spring when the new stalks formed, they were strong and hearty, sending out new, healthy foliage.

Generally, asparagus ferns like cool rooms with good air circulation and filtered sunlight or partial shade. They should be potted up in a good-quality commercial potting soil, with peat moss and ground bark or leaf mold added to ensure good drainage. You can also make your own soil by combining one part loam, one part peat moss or leaf mold and one part sharp sand. Be sure to sterilize your soil so that no pests or diseases are transferred to your new ornamentals. Always keep the soil evenly moist but never soggy. Remember, too, asparagus ferns like both spray misting and pebble trays to keep the humidity up. They do not, however, like air-conditioning, so confine them to an area without it. Feed 3 times a year, beginning in early spring. Be careful not to overfeed to compensate for lack of frequency. An occasional cup of cool tea added to the pot gives these plants a

welcome acid boost. Many of these asparagus ferns are perfect candidates for hanging baskets or areas where their cascading growth can be viewed: These arrangements will show off their beautiful arching stems. You can even take these ornamentals outdoors in the summer to a well-protected area on a deck or patio.

Yellow leaves can be caused by a lack of water, too much direct sun, or simply age. Cut the stems off close to the soil level, change the environment to meet the plant's needs of water and light, and new growth will sprout. You may also want to trim back these plants when they become too leggy. The mature ornamental asparagus will reward you with beautiful blossoms and berries.

Asparagus ferns will quickly fill a pot with their roots and you may even find the roots pushing out so hard they crack the clay. These plants prefer to be root-bound, and should be repotted only when roots fill the drainage hole. Removing the root-bound plant from the pot may prove to be very difficult as the roots tend to adhere to the surface of the pot. It may be necessary to cut the roots away from the side with a large sharp knife. Repot into a good soil mixture, like that described above, and water well. To propagate these ferns, simply divide the roots in spring and pot up the divisions. Cut back the top growth to soil level and new growth will replace it. You can also plant the berries: Pot up each berry in potting soil 1 inch deep in a 2-inch pot. This, however, is a slower, less reliable method.

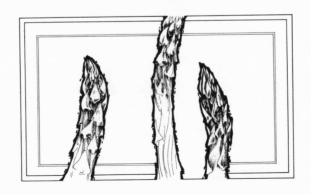

making asparagus paper

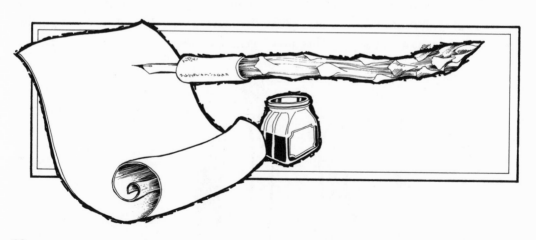

Paper can be made from the pulp of any plant. It is the cellulose which forms the cell walls of plants that provides the fibrous material needed to make paper. In the past when all paper was made by hand, pulps for papermaking varied from region to region, according to the local plants that were available. The butt ends of asparagus, so high in fiber content, are an excellent source of pulp for papermaking.

Asparagus paper is grainy textured with a slightly shiny surface. The color is a delicate, very pale green. The paper can be made in many shapes and sizes depending upon what you use to make the paper form, and the finished product can be used for decorations, invitations and stationery, as well as for collage and bookbinding projects. The method which follows makes 4-inch circles of paper. Ideas for other shapes and sizes follow the basic instructions.

EQUIPMENT

• Asparagus pulp: During the asparagus season save the butts you snap from the stalks, cut them into 1-inch pieces and freeze them until you are ready to make the paper. Then thaw the butts and place them in a blender with a small amount of water (so as not to labor the motor). Blend until they are puréed. (Two cups of asparagus butts will make 1 cup of pulp.)

• A 3-1/2 gallon container: A deep basin, such as a plastic dishpan, is best for this.

• A 6-inch square of hardware cloth (fine mesh screen).

• An embroidery hoop, 4 inches in diameter.

• A tuna fish or similar can, 4 inches in diameter, with ends removed.

• Soft cotton cloths, such as sheets, dish towels or diapers, cut in pieces about 6-inches square. These will be used to absorb the excess water from the paper. You will need about 2 dozen squares.

• A 12- by 18-inch piece of heavy cardboard or wood. This will be used as a base for the weight that rests on the paper while it is drying.

• A weight to place on the paper while it is drying to keep it flat. This can be books, bricks, concrete blocks, a typewriter, or anything similar.

THE BASIC METHOD

Fill the container with 2 gallons of warm water and add 1 cup of the asparagus pulp. Stretch the hardware cloth in the embroidery hoop and trim off the excess edges. Place the open-ended tuna can on the face of the embroidery hoop (inner part of the hoop facing down) and hold them together with both hands. The rims of these objects should be matched up evenly. This is the papermaking "form." Submerge the form in the water to the bottom of the basin, and holding it securely with both hands in a horizontal position, move the form about in the container in a circular motion. The form should always be kept in a horizontal position in the water. When the pulp is circulating well in the water, lift the form out of the water in a vertical motion. Hold the form over the container, letting the excess water drain out of the form, but keeping the can and hoop securely together.

For the next part of the process have ready the squares of cotton cloth, board and weight. You will need a flat surface such as a countertop or table, with a square of cotton cloth placed on it. Remove the tuna can from the hoop and invert the hoop on the cotton cloth so that the pulp is in contact with it. Lift the hoop slightly with both hands and slam it down firmly on the cloth, then gently lift the edge of the hoop; the asparagus paper will be left on the cotton cloth. If it does not release easily from the hardware cloth, roll a piece of dry cloth into a ball and blot the excess water from the hardware cloth. Then attempt to release the paper again. Cover the paper with a square of cotton cloth and repeat the procedure until all of the pulp is used, stacking the pieces of paper alternately with squares of cotton cloth as you go. You should end up with 8 to 10 discs of paper. The thickness of the paper sheets will vary, becoming thinner as you make more of them. If you wish to avoid this, add 1/2 cup more asparagus pulp to the water after you have made 4 or 5 pieces of paper.

Once you have stacked the sheets and put a square of cotton cloth on top, place the board on the stack and position the weight in the center of the board. In 2 or 3 hours remove the weight and the board. Remove the top blotter and place the

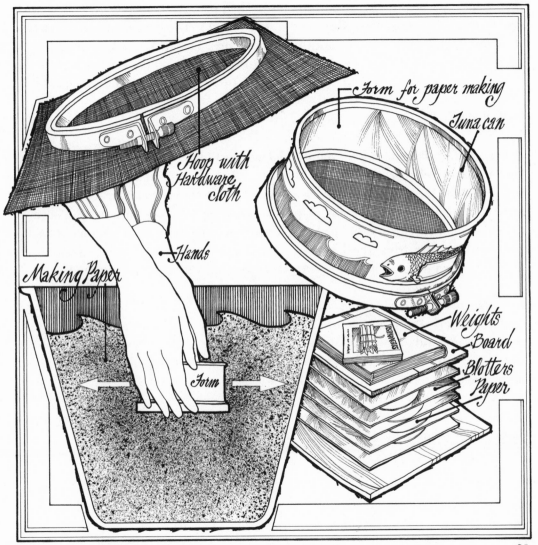

Form for paper making

Tuna can

Hoop with Hardware cloth

Hands

Making Paper

Form

Weights
Board
Blotters
Paper

91

first sheet on a dry square of cotton cloth. Then restack the paper alternately with dry squares of cotton cloth. Replace the board and weight on the new stack and let it sit for several more hours or until thoroughly dry. This final drying is necessary to keep the paper flat. Remove the squares of cotton cloth from the stack and store the asparagus paper until it is used. You will have 8 to 10 four-inch circles of paper.

PAPERMAKING VARIATIONS

Cookie Cutter Paper Choose simply shaped cutters for the best results, such as hearts, stars, bells or simple animal shapes. Use an embroidery hoop that will accommodate the size of the cutter and proceed as directed above. As the form is lifted from the water, asparagus pulp will collect in the areas between the edge of the cutter and that of the hoop. Using a sharp pointed knife, gently scrape the pulp outside the cutter from the hardware cloth before draining the excess water from the form. Then lift off the cookie cutter and proceed with the basic method.

Rectangular or Square Asparagus Paper A rectangular sheet can be made by using 2 small inexpensive wooden picture frames of the same size. With a staple gun attach the hardware cloth, stretching it tautly, to one of the frames. Proceed with the basic method. (Be sure to cut the pieces of cotton cloth in a corresponding shape about 2 inches larger than the picture frames.)

Leaves, flower blossoms or feathers can also be incorporated into the asparagus paper. Float them inside the form just before removing it from the water.

index to recipes

NANCY CLARKE HEWITT

Nancy Clarke Hewitt is an avid gardener and expert cook whose interest in asparagus ferns eventually led to this book. Since 1971 she has been a speaker on indoor plants for the University of Washington Arboretum Foundation, arranging plant workshops for the foundation units, as well as for the YWCA, private organizations and church groups. She has also written articles on indoor plants for *Sunset* and *Plants Alive* magazines. A piece on asparagus ferns in the latter evoked the suggestion that she do an entire book on asparagus and she spent the next few years collecting, testing and developing the recipes for this book. Mrs. Hewitt and her husband David live in Seattle, Washington.

RIK OLSON

An artist versatile in many media, Rik Olson received his BFA degree from California College of Arts and Crafts and later spent eight years in Europe as an arts and crafts instructor for the United States Army. While he was abroad, his graphics and photographs were widely exhibited in Germany and Italy, winning a number of awards. In addition to the Edible Garden Series, Rik Olson illustrated another book, *One Pot Meals,* for 101 Productions. He and his wife presently live in San Francisco.